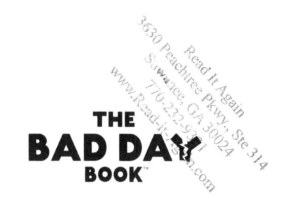

THE
BAD DAY
BOOK™

Volume 1

D1598276

The Bad Day Group, LLC
Riverton, Utah

Edited and Compiled By: Amilee Weaver Selfridge
Cover Design By: Jenalee Marshall

The Bad Day Book- Volume 1

Published and Compiled by The Bad Day Group, LLC www.thebaddaybook.com

The publisher gratefully acknowledges and credits the many individuals who granted The Bad Day Group, LLC permission to print and publish personal essays and cartoons. For the full list of authors and artist in this copyright please view the Acknowledgements Pages.

Edited by Amilee Weaver Selfridge

Cover Design by Jenalee Marshall

For Permissions contact: publisher@thebaddaygroup.com

This is a work of creative nonfiction. All of the events in this collection are true to the best of the authors' memories. Some names and identifying factors may have been changed to protect the identity of certain parties. The authors in no way represent any company, corporation, or brand, mentioned herein. The views expressed in this collection are solely those of the authors.

ISBN: 979-8-9890098-0-0

Library of Congress Control Number: 2023917770

First Edition

For Bad Days

You work so hard to Just have us laugh at you.

Contents

Introduction

The internet says to turn the water off!

There exists a universal truth. No matter who you are, where you come from, or the road you choose to travel, you will experience some bad days.

I know because I have been there. Like most people, I feel I have had my fair share of bad days.

Before I move on though, I need to specify what we mean when we say bad day. In our book (literally and figuratively), bad days come in one of two categories. Bad and terrible. Terrible days are tragic, heartbreaking, and filled with sorrow; and we will not talk

x   THE BAD DAY BOOK

about those days. We wish we could laugh those days away, but unfortunately; they are not to be laughed at. So instead, we will focus on bad days. More second-class, unpleasant, unwanted, low standard, poor quality... you get the picture.

Back to me. Like others, I feel I have had my share of bad days. If we include both the terrible and the bad—it's more than one person should need to handle. To make it easier, to take away from being overwhelmed and overburdened ... I laugh. Everything is more enjoyable when you laugh. And once I get through most of my bad days, I realize they are actually funny.

I hit a time in my life when I would share what *I* thought to be funny bad-day stories, but all I got in return was pity. This would make me wonder if I *should* be sad about my experiences, but also be sad that others thought the situation *had* to be sad. That is not a happy place to be. This led me to a new mission.

-Create a place where individuals could share their bad day experiences in a funny manner. A place where they could laugh off the frustrations and release the weight on their spirits.
-Create a place where individuals can learn that it is okay to laugh about bad situations. (Again, not terrible, just bad.) Not a place to pity or feel sorry for others.

And there lies the creation of The Bad Day Book.

A place, besides the internet, that you can turn to for bad advice and humor. A place to learn... maybe you don't have it as bad as you thought.

Welcome to The Bad Day Book.

Where we delight in ~~bad~~ funny days.

GROWING UP IN THE (CHILD) HOOD...

Are there any security cameras in the basement?

That's Going to Leave a Mark

B ACK IN THE 90S, malls were all the rage. People would flock to the malls to do all their shopping, eat, play arcades, watch movies, and even just hang out. It wasn't only for adults either. Groups of young kids would come to socialize and meet other people. Without social media to connect with others, it was the popular place to be. So, when I got invited to a birthday party at the mall, my young girl's heart just knew—it would be a memory that would last a lifetime.

To make the party even more exciting, we would participate in a mall scavenger hunt. A fun window-shopping competition. The birthday girl's parents split the large group of tween girls into two teams, each with a different list of items we needed to find within the mall and check off our list. The first team to finish their list would win prizes.

Bouncing with excitement, we all set off. Beginning on the bottom floor, weaving through the crowds, we began looking through windows to find our items as quickly as possible. We would work our way through the bottom floor, and then continue with the top floor where we would hopefully celebrate our win in the food court and arcade area. As my team found the required items and crossed them off our list, I paused for a moment to look at the next items we needed to find. Realizing I was being left behind, I looked up and started running as fast as my body could take me. I couldn't miss a second of the epic party. As I hit top speed—SPLAT.

I may have made a mistake running to catch up to the others before my eyes registered anything in front of me. And somehow, in a twist, no one, seriously no one, could explain. I ran directly into a large, no HUGE, cement pole that was straight in front of me.

This "pole" was a load-bearing cement monstrosity supporting the second floor of a *mall*. This wasn't a small pole that you could wrap your hands around. Not like a flagpole, a light pole, or even a power pole. No, this was a cement structure that could have been used to support a freeway bridge or a section of the Roman Colosseum.

And "splat" probably wasn't an appropriate description. No, it was more like the sound you would hear when standing next to the largest bell in a tiny bell tower as it rings. It is so loud your senses get confused. You start to *feel* the sound.

Well, all 500 people on the top and bottom floors of the mall *felt* the sound I made. To top it off, the splat kept echoing up and down the corridors, giving every last person at the mall an opportunity to experience the musical masterpiece I created.

As I came to... who knows if I was actually out or not? All I know is one second, I was running—then I was on the ground painfully opening my eyes to hundreds of people looking out of shop windows, hanging over the upper balcony, or running... to see me.

If people hadn't realized I caused the commotion, my small frame lying prostrate in the middle of the floor probably pointed it out. Or maybe they were drawn to the unearthly shade of my red face. If neither of those did the trick, there was no missing the bump that formed on my forehead. I had seen cartoon head injuries, always laughing at how unnaturally fast the bump would grow to an outrageous size. I didn't know that could happen in real life.

A man and woman ran towards me from the nearest shop.

As the man made it to me, he gasped in shock. "Oh wow! Look at that bump. That's going to leave a mark."

Incredulously, the woman with him replied, "I'm pretty sure it already has."

To my utmost horror, after the red drained away from my face and after I was moved to a different location, I still couldn't hide from my embarrassment. I was marked.

The prize I won during an unforgettable scavenger hunt through the mall.

A prize that almost 30 years later has still left its mark. Thankfully, though, no longer cartoon-style.

No, you can't see it (unless you are a Radiologist completing a brain MRI questioning why there is a small patch of white matter on the brain under the patient's forehead), but if you pass your hand over my forehead—you can still feel it.

Sometimes, as I stroke my "bump", as I so lovingly call it, I realize the excitement in my young girl's heart wasn't wrong.

The memory has lasted a lifetime.

-Amilee Weaver Selfridge

The Wake-Up Call

"J ON... JON...WAKE UP...GET IN HERE QUICK!"

I glared hazily at the ceiling and then stumbled out of bed. As I walked into the nursery, my wife, Kia, stared at our baby Nicole as she laughed and bounced in her crib.

Once my vision came into focus, I saw red and brown clumps that resembled spaghetti and meat sauce in Nicole's crib, on her bedsheets, and the wall. As I stepped closer, I noticed the substance in Nicole's hair, on her face, and even in her mouth. As my nostrils burned, the reality of the situation set in. "Is that...Poop?"

"Yes! Agghhhh! This is so gross! Oh, my goodness!" Kia paced the floor as Nicole laughed and cooed with glee.

Our beautiful baby girl continued to paint and layer her crib like an artist on a canvas. Although the dedication she showed to her craft was nothing short of inspirational, her final product was nothing short of disgusting.

My throat tightened. "What do we do?"

"Well, I'm gonna need you to either clean this room or bathe her. Which will it be?" Kia stood with her arms folded, awaiting my decision.

The options were very appealing, to say the least. Either take on the musty masterpiece on the crib and wall or disinfect a poop-encased infant. "Ugh, I'll just bathe her."

I reached into the crib and extracted Nicole while making sure not to allow even a drop of poop to touch me. Elbows fully extended, I rushed her down the hallway and into the bathroom. After getting Nicole into warm bath water, I grabbed her hand towel and saturated it with more soap than it could hold. My eyes locked onto the chaotic nest of hair, and then I went to work. It took until my arms ached, but eventually, the matted mess broke apart and gave way to a sea of flowing black strands. The brown bath water drained down the tub like thick mud.

I gently wiped around her mouth and cheeks. Her face, once crusted and discolored, now revealed smooth, vibrant brown skin. Nicole smiled at me and cooed as if nothing had gone wrong. After her bath, we returned to the nursery to get her dressed. To my relief, Kia finished scrubbing most of the room. The bright scent of lemon cleaning products had replaced the foul smell of the sewer system.

Afterward, Kia and I headed to the living room and crashed down on the couch. After cleaning Nicole and sanitizing the disaster zone, we enjoyed the sound of silence for the moment. However, as parents of an infant, we knew the peace wouldn't last. We knew we were destined for another beatdown at any given moment. Even though we experienced a full day's worth of chaos, the day had only just begun.

-Jon Jones

Almost Like Flying

A S A CHILD, I loved to take risks. Most of them were beyond my level of coordination. I did lopsided flips from diving boards, rode my bicycle down steep hills, and dangled headfirst from playground bars. No one ever tried to stop me. The '60s and '70s kids were free-range. Our parents didn't want to know what we were doing.

On weekends, I set my alarm for sunrise, then walked a mile to Barrie Park. Its playground was smaller than the closer one in Rehm Park and far less populated. The sandbox featured a cement wall, located above an expanse of densely packed sand. I ran towards the wall's edge and took flying leaps into the unknown. After my rump hit bottom, I rolled over, sprang to my feet, and scaled the wall again.

This exercise kept me going for hours. The weightless void thrilled me, but my body's impact reminded me of gravity's pull. Soon I was back on the wall, hurtling myself into space again. I forgot about responsibilities, the mean kids at school, and my strict but mercurial parents. If I could face the unknown with bravery and good cheer, I could deal with anything.

Usually, I performed my ritual alone. One morning, I brought a friend with me. Teresa lived on the other side of town, but we often spent Saturday nights together. I preferred to visit her enormous house, but my mother wanted to return the favor. "It's only fair," she explained. "We'll put a cot in your bedroom. The two of you can stay up as late as you want."

After setting my alarm for seven, I roused my friend. My parents were still asleep, so Teresa and I tiptoed past their door, grabbed a couple of Pop-Tarts, and headed for the park. The morning air cool and exhilarating. "Wait until you see the wall," I said. "It's so fun. You're gonna love it."

When we reached the sandbox, Teresa looked dubious. "The wall's awfully high. You jump off that thing? I'm scared."

I scoffed. "It's just a few feet. The sand acts like a cushion. I'll go first."

After scaling the wall, I ran towards the edge and soared into the air like an enormous bird. My body plummeted into the sandbox. The impact harder than I remembered, but I didn't care. "Your turn."

Teresa shook her head. "You can jump if you want. I don't think it's a good idea."

"Climb up with me," I begged. "Then you'll see how it's done."

"All right." With exaggerated caution, Teresa picked her way to the top of the wall. Usually, she was the athletic one, leaving me in the dust during gym class. *What was her problem?*

I threw myself into the sandbox again. The sand seemed even more compact than before. "See how easy it is? Just try it."

"Show me one more time. Maybe I'll reconsider."

"Nothing bad can possibly happen." I heaved myself onto the wall, took a third leap, and tumbled into the pit. My legs splayed in opposite directions. One of my kneecaps jolted against my left cheekbone. The pain was excruciating. My head bounced a couple of times, then became still.

I chuckled at the absurdity of my predicament. Hubris had gotten the best of me, as it so often did. "Well, I guess something can happen, after all." My voice sounded offhand, philosophical.

Rivulets of blood coursed down my cheek. A few crimson drops splashed onto the sand. My amusement instantly changed to horror. "Don't jump, Teresa! Come down the ladder instead."

"Don't worry, I won't jump." Teresa had never intended to leap from the wall, anyway. She lowered her body to the ground and ran over. I cradled my head in my hands, the puddle of blood widening around me. What part of my body had I damaged?

"You have a gash under your eyebrow," Teresa said.

I burst into noisy sobs. "My eyeball?"

"No, just the space between your eyebrow and the top of your eye. You must have smacked it with your kneecap."

A cluster of children hovered at the edge of the sandbox. They stared open-mouthed at the spectacle. One of the older girls dashed into the restroom and returned with a damp paper towel. Hands trembling, she extended the offering. "I'll go get my mom!" She gathered the other kids and took off running across the park.

"I think we should return to your house," Teresa said. "You might need stitches."

I pressed the towel to my face. Immediately, it turned a deep shade of red. Teresa fled towards the bathroom. She came back a moment later, carrying a gigantic clump. "These should last you a while." Teresa was a practical sort, and she loved to take charge whenever bravado failed me. "Come on, let's go."

Cursing my luck, I limped along the sidewalk. Each time I soaked a paper towel, Teresa carefully removed the dripping wad from my hands and placed it in a trashcan. Both of us hated litter-bugs. "Just a couple more blocks." Her tone was reassuring. "Your mother will know what to do."

Teresa had never been one to gloat about being right, and I loved her for it. I felt certain that my parents would still be asleep. Wouldn't they be surprised when they awoke to see me standing overhead, holding a bloodstained rag against my face? The two of them would need to make a long drive to the emergency room before they'd had the chance to drink their morning coffee.

I vowed to never jump from the wall again. It was a stupid, reckless idea, one that could only lead to ruin. Still, for a few weeks, I'd experienced the bliss of flight. That had to count for something.

-Leah Mueller

I Will Find You, Pee Smell

M Y ONE AND ONLY goal for the day was to find the source of the pee smell in the upstairs of my house. I would sit on my bed, nursing my newborn son, and catch a whiff of urine that would make my stomach turn.

Where is that coming from?! Is it a dirty diaper we forgot to throw away? Did one of the older boys wet their pants and leave them somewhere for me to find? Was this just a terrible case of bad aim?

Potty-training problems still plagued my oldest, autistic son. Distracted by ADHD, there's no time for such things as toilet breaks for my middle son. I was determined to solve the mystery by the end of the day and make my house fresh and clean again. In my best Liam Neeson voice, I said, "I will look for you, I will find you, pee smell, and I will kill you!"

Maybe a little dramatic, but I couldn't stand one more day lying in bed smelling toilet smells! I began my search under the bed. All I found there was a stash of empty Dr. Pepper cans; a conversation for another day with the four-year-old. Inhaling deeply, I ripped every sheet and pillowcase off every bed. Never had I wished for a bedwetting incident before, but I was hoping it would be that simple. Nothing. I started scouring every toy, book, and game, like some sort of drug-sniffing dog on all fours, trying to use my nose to detect the problem. I came up empty-handed again.

The overpowering scent lingered during a break to feed the crying baby. I grabbed a bottle of Febreze from my nightstand (when you live with all boys, trust me, you want Febreze on your nightstand). Carefully spraying it away from my baby's face. I hoped to inhale the fresh scent of lavender, but all I got was a whiff of a lavender-covered gas station bathroom. Time to resume my search! I checked the carpet, the shower curtains, and the bath-mats. Threw everything into the washing machine and scrubbed every nook and cranny around the toilet. The sound of the older boys fighting downstairs reached me. Oh, lunchtime! Bad move. No one wants *hangry* children. While making peanut butter sandwiches, sudden noises came from upstairs. Leaving the half-made sandwich behind, I investigated where the noise was coming from. My oldest son was playing in his room, so that left my middle son. Who was he talking to? I cracked the door open to see him with his pants and underwear on the floor, his back turned towards me. His front pointed at — not the toilet — the wall!

"What are you doing?!" I asked as I flung the door open. He turned around, midstream.

"Look, mom! I can spell my name!" he declared proudly as drops of liquid trickled down the wall...mystery solved.

-Heather G Preece

The Dubble Bubble Bubblegum Caper

I T WAS A BEAUTIFUL Sunday morning in the summer of 1955. I was six and my sister, Anita, was nine. We were physically very different. She was an intimidating figure, tall and broad. I barely came up to her chest. A stern look from Anita was a warning sign—'don't mess with me'. It was a look she had learned from our mother.

Mom stood over 5 feet 7 inches, and weighed a solid 190 pounds. She believed in 'spare the rod, spoil the child'. Anita believed in not giving her the satisfaction of crying or showing fear. Not I. Crying was my defense.

We lived in an idyllic suburb of Long Island, NY. Mom tended our large corner lot which she had filled with fruit trees and bushes. This Sunday, Mom was aggravated by the invasion of insects destroying her peach trees. A jar of the nefarious interlopers sat on the kitchen counter.

This Sunday, like every Sunday, Dad gave us a handful of coins. Anita and I were to walk the two blocks to the corner store—a combination newsstand, soda counter, and candy store. We were to purchase the Sunday Times, which the owner, Mr. Goldberg, set aside for his regular customers. We were more than happy to leave the house and our ill-humored mother behind.

We set out on our mission. On the corner, Anita stopped and declared that she had a failsafe plot to acquire the much sought-after Dubble Bubble Bubblegum, which was in a display box on the other end of the counter from the stacked Sunday Times.

"I'm going to keep talking to Mr. Goldberg while you go get the bubblegum from that box on the end of the counter."

"Steal?"

"Stop being such a wimp! Just walk down and get two pieces from the box and hide them in your pocket. It's not really stealing when it's worth less than a nickel. I'll keep Mr. Goldberg busy, and you go get the bubble gum."

She punched me in the arm. "You want the gum, don't you? You better not chicken out."

She strode ahead of me with a confidence I did not share. I hesitated at the door. Anita reached back, grabbed my arm, and propelled me ahead of her into the store. "Get going and act normal."

Not feeling very normal, I pressed up against the counter stools and slouched down, edging to the far end of the counter. My journey complete, I crouched below the counter and stared up at the bright blue and pink Dubble Bubble display box.

Anita distracted Mr. Goldberg with what she thought was scintillating conversation. Slowly, I rose to my full height and reached up over the counter until my fingers touched the rim of the display box.

Anita's plan had neglected to consider one fact: I was too short! Stretch as I might, I could not get my hand over the top of the box to grab the treasure inside. Anita glanced down the counter to see my progress. Mr. Goldberg followed her glance. There I stood, fingers dangling over the box's edge. Hearing no conversation coming from the other end of the counter, I turned. My quick assessment of the situation registered on my face.

Now, Mr. Goldberg was not a successful businessman by accident. He leaned over the counter, his face inches from Anita, and yelled.

"You trying to steal from me? You should be ashamed. Take your father's paper and get out of my store. I'm calling your parents."

Anita, shaking ever so slightly, took the paper and walked slowly out the door. I ran. As I turned the corner, I could see Mr. Goldberg through the large plate-glass window. He was on the phone.

I was in no hurry to get home. Neither was Anita. She was planning our strategy.

"Don't you say anything and don't you cry. I'll handle this."

Dang. My strategy—to cry, apologize, and swear never to do this again, had just been shot down by my sister. I resolved to hide behind Anita and hope my mother's wrath would fall entirely on her.

Mom was at the kitchen sink. My dad sat at the table sipping coffee. Something had passed between them. They also had a plan. We hesitated at the door. My dad cleared his throat and my mother turned. She crossed her arms and glared down at us. Then there was the single raised eyebrow—a sure sign of impending doom.

I must give it to Anita. She walked past my mom and handed the paper to my dad, who took it and proceeded to become absorbed in the front page. No salvation was going to come from that quarter.

Mom thwarted Anita's attempt to leave. "Stop right there, young lady! Where do you think you are going? Stealing? Anita, I know this was your idea, but Susan! I expect better from you. Mr. Goldberg is going to report you to the police tomorrow morning. I am taking you to the police station after breakfast. Now, go to your room."

We did not sleep well. Thoughts of life in striped pajamas eating gruel kept me awake. Not that I knew what gruel was, but it didn't sound appetizing. The next morning, I tried to eat our breakfast of bacon and eggs, thinking it was the last decent meal of our lives. Even Anita had little appetite. A sure sign that she was worried.

Mom was ready.

"Go get into the car. You'd better take your pajamas in case they keep you there. We are leaving for the police station in five minutes."

We piled into the back of the Buick. The fifteen-minute ride was done in silence. My sister glowered at me, arms folded and defiant. It was all my fault. I had failed!

We pulled up to an impressive building with an even more impressive guard in a green uniform. My mother told us to stay in the car and spoke with the guard on her way into the building. He approached the car, leaned down, and waved an accusing finger at us. He then turned his back and planted himself in front of our car door. We were trapped! I could not hold back my tears.

My sister commanded me. "Don't you cry! Don't you dare!"

I was a blubbering idiot when my mother returned. Anita was not.

Mom spoke briefly to the guard and entered the car. Turning to face us, she said,

"You are lucky this time. The judge was there, and he will give you one more chance. If you try to steal again, you will go to jail. And stop that crying! We are going straight to Mr. Goldberg's store, and you are going to apologize. Both of you."

I nodded, tears flinging off my cheeks. Anita stared out the window, not acknowledging my mother.

We apologized, and our Sunday trips for the newspaper resumed. Anita conducted these transactions with little conversation. I stayed in the doorway.

Many, many, many years later when Anita and I had children of our own, we were reminiscing with Mom about the time she took us to the courthouse. She laughed and confessed.

"I didn't take you to the police station. It was the state agricultural office. I needed to find out how to get rid of the bugs that were infecting the peach trees. And, of course, it was the perfect opportunity to teach two little girls a lesson,"

She smiled and raised her eyebrow.

-Susan Helene

Babysistering Month

IN THE BLISTERING SUMMER of 2018, I agreed to help my grandparents take care of my brothers in Taiwan, while my parents were both in Hong Kong. My mom was working on her new medical license and my dad was handling renovations in our peeled-paint apartment. I didn't know what I was signing up for. My brothers gleefully watched as I became a second mom to one-and-a-half-year-old Tobias. I didn't realize that I was in for an infernal arm workout routine, holding Tobias while he cried for hours, wanting my parents. And I certainly didn't know that I was going to sacrifice what I now think is the most sacred activity in life—sleeping.

But I signed up, and there Tobias was, crying one night as I tried to coax him to sleep. His fist clamped greedily around a handful of my hair like it was a rope and he was hanging off a cliff. Afraid, like always, that I would abandon him in the middle of the night. He developed this habit of clinging to me after being separated from my parents. I had to wait until he was asleep before slowly prying open his fingers. Even then, he would usually stir, that sneaky kid, in a soothed, half-asleep state just conscious enough to refasten his grasp.

I sprawled beside him, listening to the undulating buzz of bugs outside the mosquito tent and the occasional zap when one of them wandered into the blue light. Helpless in my uncomfortable position, sores settled into my neck, my shoulder, and the joint between my hip and my thigh.

At last, his breathing slowed, and his body stilled. Inch by inch, I wiggled away, careful not to nudge his hand. Holding onto my hair so that it wouldn't hurt, I pulled it out of his grip.

Free, I sighed in relief and rolled over on the bed, relaxing. My eyes drooped closed...

A wail split through the dark. I blinked away the sleep in my eyes, glancing at the neon red numbers on the digital clock. It was 2 am. Groaning, I heaved the toddler into my puny arms. My brain felt like it was stuffed with cotton and getting ripped apart by his bawling. To my surprise, he went slack, raising his arms. I lowered him onto the ground, wondering what he wanted. He grabbed my hand and tugged me out the door and down the hallway, leaning forward so much he would fall if I released him.

Sleepy, crying babies. They're the worst. They're in a bad mood and they're not rational enough to reason with. There's no bribing, no compromising, no threatening. All you can do is suffer.

By this time, he'd led me on an involuntary tour of all the rooms on that floor, and we climbed the stairs to the third floor. After we visited all the rooms there, we surveyed all the second-floor rooms again, with him still howling like his life depended on it.

"What do you want?" I growled. But his mouth was wide open, sobbing, incapable of forming a single consonant.

He's looking for Mom and Dad. The realization trickled through my muddy mind. It suddenly all made sense, the past few nights of waking up in the middle of the night. *He must've dreamed of our mom or something and started missing her. Poor kid.* Leading him back into the bedroom, I lifted him with a grunt and started rocking him, patting him on the back.

Ten minutes passed, and the crying had not faded at all. "Okay, okay, that's enough," I said. I've gone from thinking, *poor kid*, to *poor me.* "Mommy isn't here, okay?" *Just worry about it tomorrow so I can sleep.* Being nowhere near the strongest 12-year-old, my arm began hurting. I sat down on the edge of the bed and let him do his exasperating yowling.

Another ten minutes later, my arms were *really* aching. Grabbing a carrot-shaped pillow, I tucked it under my elbow so that it could rest, and kept on waiting.

By the time Tobias cried himself out, I was barely awake. My other brother had slept through the whole episode. *Jerk. I hope I'm*

your younger sibling in your next life. Then I'll show you. I dropped
Tobias down onto the pillow as gently as I could with my arms
shaking from overuse, terrified of waking him again. To my relief,
he rolled over quietly and was asleep.

Finally! Pulling the blanket over myself, I was instantly far gone
into the land of slumber.

In the end, I lasted about a month this way. My grandparents
eventually felt too sorry for me and called my mom. She quit
her job and came to take care of us. I could not—and honestly
still cannot—fathom why my parents willingly created not one,
not two, but *three* such headache-inducing problems. My parents
say that parenting is the most rewarding process someone could
go through, but let's face it: it's also the most tiring and most
permanent. A job? You can quit. A house? You can sell. A child?
Will haunt you forever.

After all, a month of dealing with one-and-a-half-year-olds is
enough to last me a lifetime!

-Kylie Wang

Best Darn Birthday Party

B Y AGE THREE, MY son had never had a birthday party. We aren't horrible parents, he just has the worst luck when it comes to birthdays. On his first birthday, we were living just outside New York City at the height of pandemic restrictions. The week before his birthday, my wife was required to take a COVID test to return to school and she tested positive. No one had symptoms, but because of the restrictions, we could not leave the house or have others over.

My son didn't notice. My wife was devastated. For months, she planned the best birthday party. A Hungry Hungry Caterpillar was the theme. We bought decorations and were planning on having people over for the first time since we welcomed our little one. All of this had to be scrapped. We had to settle for a reduced contact 'drive-by birthday celebration' where we waved at friends driving by.

The next year, my wife was determined to have the Best Darn Birthday Party to make up for the previously thwarted one. Murphy's law struck again. Just like the year before, viruses ruined our plans. This time our son came down with hand, foot and mouth disease. Again, no one had bad symptoms, but there was no party that year either.

So this year, on his third birthday, my wife was absolutely determined to celebrate THE BEST DARN BIRTHDAY PARTY. With three years of built-up excitement, my wife had a vision of what this party was going to be like. I quickly realized my best bet for survival was to ask her what she needed from me and get out of the way. Wisely, she gave me the simple task of smoking a pork butt. Or so I thought.

I woke up that Saturday morning at four to start smoking. Murphy, once again, began the mayhem. The heating element on the smoker kept tripping the fuse box. After trying multiple different outlets and unplugging different appliances, I gave up and tried plan B. I loaded the bottom of the electric smoker with charcoal and lit the pile. Not surprisingly, the electric smoker was not built to maintain a fire internally. After hours of smoking the pork butt, it still had not fully cooked. I wrapped the meat in aluminum foil and threw it in the oven for two hours. The thermometer read 170 F (77 C), but when I cut the pork open, the inside was still pink. I looked again at the thermometer after it cooled on the counter, and it still read 170 F. In desperation, I put the whole pork in the pressure cooker thirty minutes before the first guest arrived.

Thankfully, our guests were graceful enough to not show up early. We child-prepped the house as best we could, but the tiny terrors would be the true test of how well we prepared.

The meat finally finished just after the last guest arrived. We set up grazing stations of make-your-own pulled pork sliders, Mac and Cheese, and Dino chicken nuggets. Throughout the day, kids and adults would grab a bite to eat as they ran out to the backyard or returned inside to catch their breath.

Our house is small, so we tried to use the outdoor area as much as possible to accommodate our guests. The front porch had turned into the Little Tikes playground area. In the backyard, we set up a bouncy house. The box came with stakes that, of course, I did not use initially. Murphy seized the opportunity to cause chaos. A huge gust of wind lifted the bounce house with some of the smaller kids inside.

Overall, the more than a dozen kids got along well. There were the inevitable bumps and bruises, but these were all healed with kisses and ice packs. There were no restrictions on the cupcakes. We freely gave out two or three to anyone who wanted the extra dose of sugar.

After about two hours, most of the friends left. Two families ended up staying for almost three more hours. This was not a hindrance for us as the kids were playing nicely and the adults were enjoying speaking with other adults they did not work with.

As I closed the door to the last guest, I surveyed the mayhem and processed what had just happened. To my surprise, no one had broken anything. The potted plants on the back porch were laying on their side with the root balls exposed. One kid thought he was Harry Potter and was replanting Mandrakes at Hogwarts. Legos covered the floor, but putting the pieces back together is a job for another day. Overall, the destruction of the house was less than what it normally is with our two kids on a rainy day.

Looking back, I realized we stayed up too late the night before. Knowing that this was the first chance for a birthday, we felt like we had to do everything perfectly. Our son didn't have the same opinion. It thrilled our son that friends got to come over to play. He got cupcakes. Someone even brought him presents, even though we begged the parents not to.

After putting the kids down for the night, my wife smiled. The great day celebrating our son swept away the frustration from the two years prior. It was the best darn birthday party ever.

-Luke Pernotto

Dear Daughter

April 8

Dear Daughter,

I'm writing this letter for you to read in the future. Like a time capsule. You're six and don't know what that is yet. It sounds super fancy, but it's just a box full of random junk from the present day; someone with an official title buries it at a landmark in the hopes that a hundred years from now, someone will still be around to appreciate us. You don't have to wait a hundred years to open this letter. In fact, if you're reading this, I'd be shocked if you're 106. Even in the future, I assume that's old. Hopefully, you and your brother are getting on well together.

So, what are we doing here, you ask? You mean you've forgotten about your grudge already? Well, that's fair. Six is hardly old enough to hold a grudge. Not that you haven't tried. Turns out grudges don't cohabitate well with basic survival instincts. Until you have the faculties and resources to *actually* do everything on your own, you need us (your parents).

You need me.

Besides, you can't stay mad at me. Sooner than later, you'll forget why you were upset in the first place. I know this because I am also a victim of *injustice amnesia*. If only when I was six, I'd kept a time capsule–I might've remembered what crimes of humanity my parents committed against me. Since you're not thinking in terms of time capsules, I'm writing to help you out.

Let me enumerate my latest crimes:

I took your tablet away. It doesn't matter that you had an hour to get dressed for our pool getaway.

When that failed, I threatened that your mother and I would leave without you. At that point, you were much too upset to get dressed.

I confess. I committed these flagrant violations of your basic rights. I had some real nerve, didn't I? "I'll never ever go swimming with you again!" Always threatening with a consequence that hurts you instead of us. You won't always be so short-sighted, I imagine. Yet today you told me these were unforgivable offenses. Then you sought your Grandma Susan to seek validation, all while avoiding getting ready to have fun.

But what good is fun when you have legal grounds to throw a proper tantrum?

You said you'd remember this moment, but three days later, you've already forgotten all about it. I've committed more crimes, but you've likely forgotten those too. That's okay ... that's why I'm leaving you this time capsule. Treasure this always.

Now and Then,
Your Father

April 11

Dear Daughter,
I was six once.

The crimes escape my recollection, but oh, how I vividly recall *being angry*. How good it felt to express my rage to my mother. Lobbing threats in her direction that I couldn't possibly fulfill, but eager to see what would stick. Wondering what might break through her calm (bemused, even) facade. *Hint: nothing.* The more I escalated, the more she encouraged me to go on. You're wondering what I said to her, aren't you? Take notes, my dear, even though by the time you read this, it'll be much too late to act upon these nuggets of wisdom and experience.

My bedtime was either seven or eight, but probably seven. That's even earlier than we make *you* go to bed right now! My parents were hardcore. They didn't even tuck me in or wait for me to fall asleep before slipping out of my bedroom. The hour before bedtime was TV time. That's right—I had a *full hour* of screen time before bed! Bet you're feeling shorted about your 24 minutes.

Or, more likely, you've forgotten... But who knows? Anyway, an epic new show came out called *V: The Final Battle*. My mom was an old-school Trekkie, but this was something new. Exciting. Violent. All the characters were cool and unique in their own ways. For example, Diana (a member of the Visitor Earth fleet) was unique for her poofy 80s hair and adult-sized onesie.

So... when my parents committed the ultimate crime—if only I remembered what!!—I resorted to petty whining and tantrums. That had little effect, so I escalated with inspired gusto. I told my mother—the enforcer of the family—that I was an alien. A Visitor. I wasn't really human. I had lizard skin beneath my human skin. It must've shocked my mother to learn that her only child was, in fact, an imposter! But she took the news extraordinarily well, asking me to go on. Not getting the reaction I was hoping for, I let her know I would be returning home... just as soon as a ship came for me. And then my parents—but especially her—would never see me again. Expecting tears or a retraction, I paused. Nothing...

Instead, she plied me with questions and pressed for details about my origins. Where would I go? What were my plans? What would I do in the meantime?

I'd be upset, Mom! In fact, I'd never forgive you. I'd remember this moment, and once I grew up, I'd have the freedom and re-sources to rectify the situation to my satisfaction. In retrospect, I'm not sure what I'd do about it. If only I didn't suffer from this extreme case of *injustice amnesia*, I might have thought the matter through and come up with something juicy to say to my mother now.

But we're both adults now, and honestly, we'd likely find any delayed response to her crimes to be odd, out of place, or even comically ridiculous. I'm afraid to ask if she remembers what it was my parents did to draw my ire. I'm afraid knowing will spoil the memory.

Perhaps someday you'll look back and remember a defining moment of hot anger and know that your response was out of proportion to my crimes. And who knows? Maybe you'll have a good laugh.

In Solidarity,
Your Father

-Ethan Freckleton

The Wild One

"IT'S OKAY," I REASSURED my son. "Everything is going to be okay." I gently rubbed my son's curly head and took a few deep breaths.

"Wait a minute. Where's your sister?" I asked Carson, knowing that since he had just regained consciousness, he was as clueless as I was.

"Haley!"

"Haley!"

A few minutes earlier. . .

I was on the floor playing with the kids, Carson and Haley. Diagnosed with diabetes before his second birthday, Carson dealt with a slew of challenges. We met with a diabetes specialist to learn all we needed to care for our chronically ill toddler. The educator overwhelmed us with the needed information and warned us about diabetic scenarios that might arise. As thorough as she was, however, she never warned us about how the disease might affect Carson's sibling, Haley.

Haley is 22 months younger than Carson, and she came out of the womb with an agenda. As soon as she learned to crawl, she was getting into everything. Things only worsened when she learned to walk, which, of course, she started at only 8 months old. As the baby in the family, she demanded to be at the center of all attention. If she couldn't be, then we knew she was somewhere, doing something forbidden.

As we were playing on the floor, suddenly, Carson passed out. Because his blood sugar was rarely within range, he would sometimes pass out when his sugar got too low. I tried to wake him up and get him to drink some juice, but he wouldn't budge. This meant that I needed to get his glucagon and give him a sugar shot.

I went into panic mode and focused my full attention on bringing Carson back to consciousness. Sometimes, what a mother sees as a crisis, a child sees as an opportunity; so was the case with Haley. Everywhere she looked, she saw adventure, and with every adventure she took, I got another grey hair.

While I was handling the crisis at hand, Haley snuck off. It wasn't until Carson came back to consciousness that I noticed she was missing.

"Haley!" I called. No response. "Haley, where are you?" More silence.

It was after the third time I called that I finally got a response, but it wasn't from Haley. Instead, our dog, Sadie, came running to my call. Trotting lightly and wagging her tail, Sadie ran up the hall to greet me. Something wasn't right. *How did you get wet?* Touching her slicked black hair, I realized it wasn't water – she was covered in Vaseline.

My second panic mode of the day kicked in as I recalled hearing that Vaseline could be poisonous for children if they ate it. *What if Haley ate it?* I ran in the direction Sadie had come and found a happy Haley rubbing herself with Vaseline. Her canvas had run out, so she used herself for her art.

Fortunately, at the end of the day, all was well. Carson recovered from his low blood sugar, and Haley did not ingest petroleum jelly. The dog, however, was another story. I gave her a bath every day for a week and a half before I got all of the Vaseline out. When I look in the mirror and see the grey overtaking the brown in my hair, I know that a few of those grey hairs came from the time my daughter jellied the family dog.

-Tammy Brown

Poopy Night

AT TWO AND A half, Evelyn was still in pull-ups. Blame it on the long working hours, the divorce, or me being a first-time mom, but she was not yet potty trained. On Monday nights, I made my long commute to California State University, Northridge, to teach Advanced Argumentation and Deliberation to seniors and master's students who rarely wanted to argue or deliberate.

Unbeknownst to me, my boyfriend, Jordan, was terrified of dirty diaper changes. Apparently, he spent most of his Mondays praying for only wet diapers before watching her for me. One Monday night, he realized his worst fear had arrived: a poopy diaper. As he attempted a smooth, clean change, she looked into his eyes, gleefully declaring, "Daddy, look at my poop!" She slapped her hands between her legs and distributed her poop to her hands, her face, and my boyfriend's face. After struggling through an entire package of wipes, Jordan gave up and threw her in the bath to finish the job.

After Evelyn's bedtime, feeling a bit more confident and relieved, he sat to watch a movie and relax. He went to bite a fingernail.... And immediately regretted it.

-CLS Sandoval

Schooled in Life...

This isn't good. She replaced all my grades with crying emojis.

Deadline

I T WAS THE DAY after the deadline for the term paper submission. I found myself reminding my students of the terms of our agreement regarding the format, word count, and submission date. We all agreed that the online submission site wouldn't be accepting any more term papers after that designated deadline. They forced me to put my foot down on those who kept on shoving their printed copies at me during class.

While explaining deadlines one student shot her hand up.

"Sir," she said, "I was ready to turn over my term paper last night, but the submission site suddenly closed."

"And what time did you try submitting?" I said.

"Five after ten."

"But we did agree that the deadline was at exactly ten p.m., right?"

The room became suddenly quiet after that. I was about to continue giving other reminders, but her hand shot up again. This time, she stood up as I addressed her.

"But, sir," she said, "Aren't deadlines supposed to be on a time or day by which something must be done?"

"Yes," I said casually, "And that was March 5, at ten pm."

Then, I said with a little emphasis, "Last night."

"Sir," she insisted, "You must have misunderstood me."

I got to say I was getting annoyed at this point. But being a teacher, one has to have more patience with students. So, I took a deep breath and humored her.

"Please," I said, "tell me."

"When I finished my term paper," she said, "I knew the day wasn't over until twelve in the morning. Sir, this means I should still have been given time to submit my paper."

"Again," I said, my patience almost running thin, "We all agreed the deadline would be at ten p.m. That's enough time for me to check all the papers in your section before I sleep."

"Sir, wait," she said.

She rummaged through her bag with nearly half of the class looking at her. A few of them sigh. I honestly was curious by this point. What I didn't expect was her pulling a big dictionary in front of me. She took a deep breath, opened to a bookmarked page, and read aloud, "Sir, according to this dictionary, a deadline is a date or time before which something must be done."

"Also," she continued, "it is the time after which copy is not accepted for a particular issue of a publication."

"So, sir," she said with grave deliberation, "based on this meaning; you should still accept my term paper because I already mentioned I finished it last night. If not for your online submission site, we wouldn't be discussing this matter right now."

Somewhere, I heard a groan.

I looked at her sympathetically and said, "First of all, that's the university's portal. We're all required to use it. Second," and this time I gave her the nicest smile I can muster, "Again, what day is it today?"

"March 6," she said, glaring at me.

"Yes," I said, "And not March 5, so still that's a no."

She was already breathing heavily when she sat down.

"You know," I sighed, "I just hope you meet a boss with greater patience than I have in you."

I waited... No response.

I could finally continue to my lesson.

-Bien Santillan Mabbayad

The Halloween Hump

I N 1975, I LANDED my first job as a grade three teacher in the east end of Toronto, Canada. I recall this group of guinea pigs with a mixture of nostalgia and horror.

My classroom was part of a new initiative, heralded as open-concept teaching. They expected the teachers to mix grades, team-teach, and rotate small groups of students according to interests and ability levels. All while sharing spaces with no walls to divide the classes. On day one, my students filed in, eyeing me with curiosity. Neighboring teachers yanked partitions to new positions to block auditory and visual distractions. There was a vast discrepancy between theory and reality.

"Let's be quiet, so we don't disturb other classes." My broken-record pleas continued to be ineffective.

When autumn leaves carpeted the earth, skeletons, ghosts, and ghouls decorated the surrounding classroom walls. Mine looked barren. I had an inspiration. I'd buy five of the biggest pumpkins at a local market. Monday at lunchtime, I rushed to the corner market, made my purchase, and lugged one cumbersome, orange sphere up three agonizing flights to my class. Each day brought mounting excitement as, one by one, I displayed them on the art table. My back shrieked in agony, but the excited babble of my students made it worthwhile. By Friday afternoon, the kids were bouncy balls of anticipation as I divided them into five pumpkin-decorating groups.

"Please keep your voices down," I rasped for the millionth time. "Use the big spoons and get all the pulp and seeds out. Then draw a scary face for me to carve."

Competitive scooping erupted into a thunderous roar. Orange goop was tossed everywhere, missing the inadequate layer of protective newspapers. Up to their elbows, they embarked on a slime-throwing fight.

"Sit on your bottoms, hands on your laps!" I bellowed.

Stunned by my explosion, they obeyed. Teachers glared and pulled partitions, hoping to shut me out. After five minutes, the kids were squirming, itching to get back at it. "Remember to keep your voices quiet," I implored in a fake mellow tone.

Each team sketched a grimacing face with markers. I raced around, sawing at the shells with a serrated knife and distributing scrap paper, cotton batons, fabric, yarn, old hats, scarves, and carrots. Enervated by my "little artists," I circulated amidst the mayhem to shout unheard words of encouragement. Teachers poked heads around partitions to glower. I pretended not to see them. As we completed our jack-o'-lanterns, the students whooped with pride. I captured their masterpieces with my camera.

"Let's light candles and put them inside!" shouted George, the class activist. The rest of the students cheered in approval.

"Setting fires is NOT a good idea!"

The children, upset that I'd vetoed their exciting idea, ignored my hoarse commands to clean up.

At day's end, they stampeded out of the class and down the stairwell, their shrieks echoing off the walls. An irate caretaker muttered under his breath as he shoved the vacuum back and forth over layers of slimy seeds.

The following Monday morning, after an unusually warm Indian-summer weekend, I mounted the stairs to my class. A foul odor intensified the higher I climbed. All the jack-o-lanterns had rotted, forming a Salvador Dali array of gruesome faces. The miffed caretaker helped me scoop the fetid remains into garbage bags.

"What were you thinking?" he muttered, hoisting the bags over his shoulder.

The students arrived.

"Where are our pumpkins?"

"Who stole them?"

"What's that awful smell?"

It took a long time to settle them. I passed tissue to the criers and promised an upcoming Halloween party as amends for the putrefied pumpkins.

On the big day, we joined a school-wide throng to parade around the block and admire one another's costumes. I wore a hooded housecoat and yanked a suffocating monster-mask over my head. My students roared in approval, and we began our trek. As we merged with other classes, a tiny kindergarten girl dressed as a fairy sprite peered at me and howled in terror.

"It's okay, honey!" I said in a muffled voice, hurrying to remove the disguise. Lurching in circles, I tugged at the mask. It finally released its hold on my sweaty head.

Too late. The horrified child broke ranks and raced toward the street and oncoming traffic. Her teacher ran after her, grabbed her hand, pulled her back to safety, and fired me a look of frustration. I apologized, hid the mask under my housecoat, and did a walk of shame.

After the parade, my throng stampeded back to class for the promised party. We gorged on candy kisses and chocolate. High on sugar, the more energetic in the group began a game of tag, racing around the desks to steal one another's treats. My roars of disapproval once again attracted the unwanted attention of several colleagues. I wondered if I was doomed to fail the two-year teacher probation period.

At dismissal, I surrendered my usual routine of lining them up, and watched, weary-eyed, as they raced out without tidying up. I picked up the trash as best I could and left early to avoid the caretaker. On the long subway ride home, I napped. I had scaled and survived the Halloween hump. Two months down, eight to go until the end of June.

-Victoria MacDonald

How They Ended Upside Down and Dead

I was fresh from having graduated college with a B.S. in Education. After doing nothing for two months, I was running low on cash and opted to take a position as a sixth-grade teacher in a small town in Massachusetts.

The school was built during World War I. It wasn't until I attended an orientation meeting for the staff that I discovered some disturbing facts about my new job. There were only ten classrooms (three 4th grade, three 5th grade, and four 6th grade). Eight of us were first-year teachers. This meant that seven left (escaped?) and the superintendent promoted one to principal. It didn't take long to discover the reason for the exodus.

The aging, two-story building did not have air-conditioning, did not have screens on the windows, and was next to a large free-range chicken farm. Each of my classes had thirty-five students. The school lacked a gym and a PE teacher. As a result, when the weather prevented holding gym classes outside, I had to entertain the kids in my cramped classroom with jumping jacks, bean bags, etc.

Then there was the telephone. The principal, Mr. Kelso, was also the principal of a four-room school located a half mile away. He split his time between the two schools, as did the lone secretary. When they were away from the school, the phone calls came into my room.

Ring.

"This is Mr. Drewniak."

"Yes, would you tell Mary to have the bus driver drop her off at Granny's this afternoon?"

"Yes, I will."

"Please don't forget."

"I won't. Goodbye."

"Hello, is Mr. Kelso there?"

And on-and-on it went.

Day one. Male staff members were required to wear a suit jacket, long-sleeve white shirts, and narrow ties. Underwear seemed to be optional.

I arrived early — 7:15. Buses rolled in just before 8:00. Classes began at 8:15.

I drew bus monitoring duty. Kelso explained my duties. "The buses will drive to the back of the school. As the students exit the buses, direct them to the playground and have them line up when the bell rings. Most of the fifth and sixth-graders will know what to do. I will come out and help with lining up the fourth-grade pupils."

Sounds easy enough.

The driveway was horseshoe-shaped. In came the first bus. I was standing about five feet from the bus door. Big mistake! The first student, a sixth-grader nicknamed Titanic, came running off the bus. Blam! Down I went, flat on my back. Within seconds, I was surrounded by three to four dozen amused eleven and twelve-year-olds.

"Is he okay?"

"Is he dead?"

"Hey Titanic, you're in big trouble."

Meanwhile, Titanic kept repeating, "Are you okay? I'm sorry! I'm sorry..."

I was unhurt physically, but my mental state was in shambles. Jumping up, I assured him I was okay and told him it was my fault for standing too close to the bus.

By 9:00, the temperature in my classroom was 86 F (30 C) and it was humid. There were dozens of chicken farm flies buzzing around our room. But, if I had closed the windows, the temperature in the room would soar to over one hundred. The student desks were relics with empty inkwells. Some boys came prepared with heavy-duty rubber bands and were trying to zap the flies and stuff the dead ones into the inkwells.

I quickly put an end to that. "If I see even one rubber band tomorrow, I will triple your homework. Got it?"

By the sounding of the dismissal bell, the temperature was in the low 90s. Flies were everywhere. It was then that my Polish intellect kicked into overdrive and drummed up a solution to the fly problem. I flagged down the custodian and nailed a can of insect spray. Back in the classroom, I closed all the windows and emptied the spray.

My plan was foolproof (or so I thought). On the way home, I sprung for a large fan to help circulate the air in the classroom and more fly killer. I arrived early the next morning, ready to put my plan into action. There wasn't a fly — alive or dead — to be seen. The custodian had thoroughly swept the room. I opened the windows halfway and sprayed each window around the opening. Fan on, I was ready to rock and roll.

Genius, pure genius, Don.

Kelso walked into my room before the start of classes.

"Well, Mr. Drewniak, how did your day go yester..."

He clutched his chest. His face and the top of his bald head quickly turned a crimson red as he stared at the area behind me.

Oh no, he's having a heart attack!

"Eighteen years! Eighteen years I had them, and nothing happened. You're here one day and you murdered all of them! Gone! My precious Nellie and Katie and Roger Dodger and..."

Drats, the goldfish tank!

I turned around and stared in panic at the glass tank that was tucked into the corner of the room. Around three dozen fish were floating upside down in the tank. The insect spray had poisoned them. Four boys walked into the room a few minutes later and removed the tank.

Kelso never forgave me for the "murdering" (as he repeatedly called it) his cherished fish. As a result, we had a stormy relationship.

Two summers later when I informed him that I was being drafted into the U.S. Army (thanks to Lyndon B. Johnson's Vietnam War), I am certain he spent the night celebrating.

-Don Drewniak

The Lecture

FOUR SLIDES INTO THE day's presentation, I found myself distracted by the mousy girl in the front row who was busily poking through her purse. My mentor had told me, "If a student isn't paying attention, don't make a big deal of it, just say the student's name to bring their attention back to the presentation". Only I'd forgotten her name. June? Jane? Julia?

Something "J", but it wouldn't come and I needed to focus on what I was saying. I plowed ahead with one of my better anecdotes about today's topic; watching out of the corner of my eye as she retrieved first a pen, and then a pad of yellow Post-it notes, from the depths of her bag. Forgotten her laptop? Well, a Post-it pad was better than nothing, I thought, glad the distraction was now over. I paused for the students to laugh as I finished the anecdote. It seemed to have gone over well.

J-girl was scribbling furiously, no doubt desperate to catch up.

I clicked ahead to the next slide, talking to the listed points but not reading them out. "Your students can read," my mentor had insisted. "So don't bore them. Use the slides to keep yourself organized, to highlight the key points for their notes; but what you're saying can't duplicate what they're reading, or they'll stop listening."

Common sense, really.

My mentor had been the only instructor in the Education Faculty worth listening to. No incomprehensible Derrida essays, no hopelessly outdated Dewey 'Progressivism', no useless lectures on developmental psychology. Just 750 Teacher's Survival Tips. Practical advice I applied in every moment of my teaching.

J-girl finished writing and was pushing the yellow sticky in my direction.

"Hold your questions 'til we get through to the end of this bit," I told the class, as a couple of other hands went up. "The next two slides will likely give you your answers." I clicked for the next slide.

J-girl shoved the yellow sticky off her desk and onto the empty desk directly in front of me. I thought that a bit pushy after I had just told the class to hold their questions. I ignored her and spoke to the slide.

She sprawled forward, extending her arm to its fullest. Pushing the very edge of the yellow-sticky with her fingertips until it was almost falling off the front of the desk as I stood one row over.

Why couldn't the girl take a hint? I was not taking questions until I finished with the next slide. The slide after that one was actually titled "Any questions?", over a cartoon of a class with all their hands up. That's where there was a natural break for questions. Why couldn't students trust me to pace things?

As I spoke to the last bullet on the current slide, J-girl half stood out of her desk, still holding the yellow sticky at arm's length, but now waving it slowly up and down. I had to dig deep to find the patience not to show my annoyance. How entitled did a student have to be to interrupt the speaker mid-flow—put their own needs ahead of the entire class, really?

"Always take student input as soon as it comes up," my mentor's voice said in my head. "What one student is wondering, they all want to know. They have to feel some ownership over airtime or they'll tune out!"

I huffed out a sigh. Right as always, professor. But I don't have to like it.

I reached down, snatched the yellow stickie out of her hand, and read it aloud:

"Your fly is open."

-Robert Runté, PhD

The Promise

I WOKE UP THAT fateful day immersed in anxiety and misery. How would I survive what lay ahead?

It was 1959, my junior year in college, and I was studying to become a teacher. I loved it and thrived in the preparations I was making to become a professional educator. Classes in English, Psychology, Reading Methods and more gave me no problems. What loomed ahead on this awful day, however, made me shiver with fear.

No way out. As I dragged my reluctant body from the warm cocoon of blankets, I told myself I had to face the music. Face the music? That was exactly what I had to do this morning. My churning stomach meant no breakfast today. Each tick of the clock brought me closer to disaster.

I donned a coat and gloves, wrapped a scarf around my neck, and set out on legs that felt heavier with each step. For once, I didn't relish the walk across campus. Face the music? I shuddered as that simple phrase skipped through my mind once again. Slowly, I journeyed to the final exam in my Music For The Elementary School class...an exam with no paper and pencil. I might have done all right with a test like that. Instead, the professor would select any three songs of the nine we were to learn to play on the piano. The pieces were not concertos or etudes. These were little children's songs, like "Mary Had a Little Lamb".

The first week of class the professor explained that we had to learn three groups of songs in three different keys. To be sure, we had all semester to do this. Plenty of time to master them, he assured us. Music Department pianos were available for practice.

"Piece of cake," the girl next to me said.

"Easy enough," another chirped as I glared at her.

"Cinch class," yet another said, rolling her eyes to Heaven.

I kept my silence, but the worry started. Music was not one of my many talents. I enjoy listening to music and can appreciate it. But I could not learn to tap a triangle at the right time in third grade, could not sing on key, and could not read the musical notes on a staff. No musical aptitude—whatsoever.

I signed up for practice times several days each week all semester. Anyone nearby must have winced at my efforts. Lovely songs tripped off the fingers of other practicing pianists, music floating through the hallway.

I asked my roommate for help. After several sessions, she told me it was a hopeless cause and suggested I cry on the professor's shoulder, plead for mercy or something more drastic. What the more drastic might be, I feared to ask.

I did talk to the professor, poured out my tale of woe. I explained I was "Musically Handicapped."

"Have you put some effort into this?" he asked me. "Really put some work into learning to play these little songs on the piano?"

With tears threatening, I assured him I had. His answer was that I would do fine when the time came, and he strode out of the classroom after patting me on the shoulder.

Now, the day of my demise had arrived. I could not have feared execution any more than I did this music exam.

The professor greeted me with a smile, rubbed his hands together and said, "Well now, are we ready?"

I sank onto the bench and attempted to play the three songs he selected. He kindly picked what were probably the three easiest pieces...and I managed to butcher each one.

At the end of my futile performance, the professor beckoned me to his desk. He looked at me, started speaking, then stopped and wiped his hand across his forehead. "Nancy, this is what we are going to do. You've put forth a great deal of effort, so I will give you a C in this class on one condition."

"Anything," I answered.

"You must promise me you will only teach in a school that also employs a music teacher!" He grinned at me after making the statement.

With vast relief, I made the promise.

I taught in more than one school district, but I always made sure it was one that had a music teacher. I watched with great admiration as music class was conducted, and as songs were played on the piano the teacher rolled from classroom to classroom twice each week. What a genius she is, I thought, as her fingers flew across the keys.

To this day, the only musical thing I play is a CD player or radio. After all, a promise is meant to be honored.

-Nancy Julien Kopp

You've Never Seen a Cow Before

ONE DAY IN ART class, the teacher asked me to draw a cow. Seemed like no problem at all. I've seen them before. As I put my drawing up, my stomach dropped. The teacher got to my drawing. "So, you've never seen a cow before?"

I cringed in my seat. I guess not. Oh well, I still passed the class.

-Braden Lewis

Toga Tale

M Y SIXTH GRADERS WERE more excited than usual this morning. We had just read *Detectives in Togas*, a children's novel set in Ancient Rome concerning a mystery that a ten-year-old solved. The students were acting out a scene in costume. The students spent time designing a Roman Temple background. White sheets, as togas, were draped around the main actors. The children in the chorus were equally excited, as they all corroborated in writing the scene. I had the video camera ready to film the short episode.

One actor brought in handcuffs to use as a prop. All this was unknown to me! As the scene unfolded, one child placed the handcuff on a very slim girl, Julie. As the group was acting out the scene, she became more and more agitated. I realized what was happening and intervened. Julie raised her arm and cried, as she could not remove the cuffs. I asked the boy who brought in the handcuffs,

"Why did you bring these in for the play? Where is the key?"

"I think I left it home."

More tears.

We called the boy's mother, and she came into the school, rattled but without the key.

Lots of crying ensued.

In the meantime, the mother stayed with the class as I took the child into the bathroom and used liquid soap on her wrist to help slide the cuffs off her arm. However, I did not want to yank the cuffs off if it would hurt the child. After that, there were more tears from the little girl and the other children. Also, time was running out for the students to move to the next class. What to do?

The sixth graders were not the only ones feeling frustrated. Outwardly calm, frustration and fear were slowly overcoming my resolve. Finally, I called in the troops. The head janitor and two others came down the hall to my classroom with a large wrench and long pin. All the while, I heard the theme song from *Bonanza*, a 1950s western. He took the handcuff in hand and worked the pin in the lock. After a few minutes, it opened. The cuffs fell off. Tears subsided as the entire room broke out into applause. I let out a thankful sigh and thanked the champion of the day.

When alerting the principal of the situation, he shook his head with a smile, "In all my years in education, I have never witnessed this kind of situation."

No one got hurt and the school schedule moved on as scheduled. It all ended well. I never planned this type of activity again, with or without a video. The next day, I asked the boy who brought in the handcuffs why he did that. He had no answer.

-Rosemary McKinley

But it Looked Like the Right Ingredient...

F OR 20 YEARS, I had the privilege of teaching high school students about all aspects of restaurant operations. It was a vocational class called "Food Services" and was very similar to culinary arts. Naturally, the students always preferred time in the kitchen as opposed to classroom work.

One of the first recipes I would have them attempt to make was chocolate chip cookies from scratch. My reasoning was simple. Almost everybody likes them, but more importantly, it taught them the valuable lesson of adhering to the recipe instead of skipping preparation steps. The cookies had four stages of prep, involving three mixing bowls. This was great for dividing the class into groups of three or four and giving everyone something to do.

One year, the class set about to make the chocolate chip cookie recipe. A group of four boys had a student, Chris, whom I appreciated for his enthusiasm and sunny disposition; even when dealing with the distractions caused by his attention deficit disorder.

After the classroom instruction time, the students went into the kitchen and worked through the various stages of creating the cookie dough. They then shaped the dough into individual cookies, put them on commercial sheet pans, and placed those into the oven. As the cookies baked and cooled, students would clean up anticipating the "testing" stage of the daily lesson.

As the class sat down to enjoy the fruits of their labor, students in Chris's group made faces and comments showing displeasure. "These cookies taste funny, Mr. Craft." I asked them to bring me one and with one bite I detected a salty, Unami quality which is usually absent from sweet, baked goods.

Over the years, I found mistakes were better learning moments than something that goes perfectly right the first time. So, we went over the recipe and each of the four students explained to me what they had each done. Chris told me he was responsible for adding the last ingredients to the dough, which included vanilla flavoring. I asked him to show me specifically what he used. He went and grabbed a gallon container of a dark brown liquid that looked like vanilla. As he stood smiling, holding the liquid flavoring agent, I quickly surmised the problem. He had picked up a container without checking the label and was holding a gallon of Worcestershire Sauce! When I explained the importance of reading the product label and how one wrong ingredient drastically changed the flavor of the end product; his group looked at each other and nervously laughed.

Assuming the lesson was over, I grabbed the sheet pan of cookies and headed for the 55-gallon kitchen trash container. "Whoa, whoa!" One of them shouted. "What are you going to do with those?" I told them I was throwing them out — "We'll eat them! Don't throw them out!"

Not only did four students, which included one very impetuous young man, learn a valuable cooking lesson that day, but I was able to share the story (name redacted of course!) with future classes to help prevent them from making a similar mistake.

-William Craft

Tadpole Heaven

C HANGE IS AN INEVITABLE and important part of life. When I brought live tadpoles into my classroom, that was the lesson I had planned to teach. Too bad it didn't turn out that way.

These were not ordinary tadpoles like the tiny ones I collected as a child. They were large, green, bullfrog tadpoles I had purchased at the local Walmart for a whopping forty-nine cents apiece. "Oh, they're easy to care for," the young salesgirl assured me as she placed the precious cargo in a see-through plastic bag. The tadpoles eyed me warily with big, bulbous eyes, and I smiled back confidently.

Sure, I could raise them. I had a rabbit and crickets in my classroom, didn't I? Tadpoles would be a cinch, a snap! Yeah right.

I placed the tadpoles in an aquarium filled with water and colored rocks (primary colors at that). For a while, the tadpoles swam about, enjoying their new home.

After a few days, the children complained, "The water smells funny!"

I knew I needed to take care of it that day or walk into the smell of a fish market the next morning, I placed the tadpoles in a bowl and poured out the filmy water. Then I filled a bucket with fresh water and poured it into the aquarium.

The next morning, the tadpoles seemed listless and depressed. I threw in some food and kept my fingers crossed. But by the time the children returned to the classroom one of them tugged at my sleeve and announced. "Teacher, the tadpoles are standing up!"

I walked over and, sure enough, the tadpoles looked like tiny green soldiers at attention with their noses pressed against the waterline. "Hmm," I replied nonchalantly even though my heart raced, "Maybe they lined up to go to lunch." The child nodded thoughtfully and continued to study them.

As soon as the last child left for the day, I rushed to the gravesite. I found our "new amphibian friends" still modeling correct posture in the now murky green water.

I've seen dead fish before, but never a tadpole! When I was six, I pet one of my father's prized Black Angels. The next morning it lay on top of the aerated water glaring accusingly at me with its one visible fishy eye.

Forty years of guilt dragged me back to my parents' living room in McKinney, Texas. Reluctantly, I picked up the largest tadpole and laid it in my hand. It didn't squirm or wiggle but lay in sweet repose and (dare I say it?) at still as D-E-A-T-H!!!

"Oh," I moaned – a full-blown panic attack setting in. How would I explain this to twenty-two five-year-olds who trusted me implicitly?

After cleaning out the aquarium and flushing the tadpoles the way that many good little tadpoles go, I called my "lifeline" – Walmart.

This time an older, more experienced saleslady helped me. I told her step by step what I had done to care for them.

"Well, honey," she said, "Was there soap or some kind of cleaner in the bucket?"

I shuddered. Only a few months before, I had mixed bubble solution in that very same deathtrap complete with three tablespoons of glycerin. Once again, I could feel the accusatory fish eye glaring at me down through the years.

The next day the children assailed me with, "Where are the tadpoles?"

Should I lie? NO! Make up a story? NO! I had to tell them the truth.

"Oh, they went to tadpole heaven last night," I replied, fudging the truth just a little.

"But where is tadpole heaven?" One of my brighter (and obnoxious) students asked. Sure-tie the noose good and tight!

I envisioned the swirling water as the tadpoles received their sailor's burial. I could not bring myself to divulge that much information. "Well, it's a nice, cool place where they'll never be sick again."

Then I took a deep breath and began to explain environmental pollution to a classroom full of anxious young biologists.

-Becky Villareal

Who Wants Free Cola?

I T WAS A NORMAL day in the Philippines. When I say normal, I mean hot, humid, and draining. Doctors recommend drinking 8–10 glasses of water. In the Philippines, we drink 15-20.

As a student, I actively participated in school activities, which included being elected as class president. Class officers in the Philippines are not about planning for projects or programs. No, it's about being the teacher's buddy and facilitating a disciplined classroom setup. You help clean the classroom, clean the assigned sector outside the classroom, and take out the garbage. So yeah, it's about cleaning, cleaning, and more cleaning.

It's a good thing that our cafeteria offers fresh and carbonated drinks. And if you don't have money to buy those, we always have two jugs of free water in the cafeteria.

One day, I was so tired that my co-officers and I went to the cafeteria to avail ourselves of free water. You can imagine our surprise when we noticed the jug was still heavy, yet no water was pouring into our glasses. We wondered why.

Is it physics? Are we tired—so tired we're imagining things? Maybe there was a ghost playing around.

Our Vice President shook the jug and heard rattling sounds from the inside. When checking what it might be, we all looked at each other in surprise. As a substitute for ice, bottles of frozen Coca-Cola and mineral water were making the water colder. Fortunately, they were unopened bottles. You can imagine the look on the faces of my co-officers upon making the big discovery. It was very disgusting.

Soon, more students noticed our ruckus at the water station, commented about how disgusting it was, and asked why the management even thought of doing it. Being the class officer that I am, I tried to talk to the cafeteria manager about it, giving them the benefit of the doubt, that they just made a mistake.

When I asked her, she answered as if it were a normal thing to do. She said they forgot to make ice. In the Philippines, we don't use ice cubes that much. We put water in a small plastic bag, tie it, and freeze that to make ice. Then we put that ice bag in the jug to make the water colder. If we need smaller portions of ice, we crush it. When they saw the frozen cola and water, they put it inside the jug to make the FREE water colder. Yes, she emphasized the word free, as if we owed her for making the FREE water colder.

It was crazy! Instead of owning up to their mistake, she justified and defended their action. In the end, we were mad, tired, and thirsty.

The next afternoon I went back to check. And voila! The jug was there, with cold water pouring from it and frozen Cola bottles inside. Disgusting!

As officers, we talked about the right course of action for this issue. One of my peers gave a suggestion. Write to the administration and let them handle it. But I have a better idea.

"Who wants free coke?" I asked.

You could see the smiles on their faces.

For the rest of the week, we got free cola from the filthy water jug. It was cold, refreshing, and best of all—IT WAS FREE!

Soon after, a few students followed our example. One day the jugs were emptied.

Someone said they heard the cafeteria manager getting mad at her employees. One employee wanted to report the students who stole their products. Another said that would mean admitting everything to everyone...even the "frozen bottles" part.

The next Monday afternoon, the jugs were filled with water, lukewarm.

-NRV

Going Fishing

NEAR THE END OF a wild ride during my first year of teaching, I announced a Field Trip to my 4th-grade students. "We are going to take a bus to downtown Chicago, where we will visit the Shedd Aquarium and then have a boat ride on Lake Michigan."

Whoops and hollers greeted the announcement. My experimental class of 21 emotionally troubled kids liked field trips as much as any other students did. It would be a day off from school and maybe they'd learn something, too.

Having 10 very aggressive students and 11 seriously withdrawn students had tested me throughout the school year. We also had to deal with "New Math" that year in 1961. It presented a whole different way of grasping the traditional facts and figures these kids learned in the first three grades. We struggled together as I, too, had to learn the new methods.

When I told the class about the field trip, I noticed Donnie stopped doodling in his notebook. He sat up straighter in his desk and gave me full attention. Rather unusual for this intelligent boy who had a major problem with reading. Unless the reading material was about Africa or anything African. Then, he could read perfectly.

Later that morning, when the class was busy doing multiplication worksheets, Donnie strolled up to me. He shoved back the shock of hair always on his forehead, then leaned both elbows on the edge of the desk, hands under his chin. Eyes twinkling, he said, "When we go to the aquarium, I'm going fishing." Then silence.

"No Donnie, we don't fish at the aquarium; we look at fish and learn about the many kinds they house there."

He sauntered back to his desk and started on his math worksheet. I noted a little smile on his face as he worked.

At least once every day prior to the field trip, Donnie repeated his "I'm going fishing." statement to me. No more, no less. And each time, I repeated my answer. He'd lope back to his desk, grin wider each day.

Excitement reigned on Field Trip day as my class filed out the big double doors of our suburban school and boarded the bus. After an hour's ride, we reached the famed Shedd Aquarium on the Chicago lakefront. Two of my students' mothers volunteered to help on this special day. One led the children from the bus to the entryway and the other stayed about mid-way through the group. I brought up the rear.

Donnie had been in the middle of the group, but he let the others go by until he was near the end of the line. Suited me fine, as I could keep an eye on him. As we neared the entryway, a fellow teacher from one of the other fourth grades hailed me. I went over to see what she wanted, then hurried after the rapidly disappearing line of my students.

I was the last one to go through the revolving door into the lobby area of the aquarium. The first thing that caught my eye was a lovely, large pond and garden area filled with lush vegetation. A waist-high wrought-iron fence circled the area. Fish of all kinds darting through the water. The second thing I noted was Donnie, feet on the bottom rung of the fence, leaning over with a long string that ended in a fishhook. As his arm went back above his head, ready to spin his line right into the pond, two things happened.

My heart did a double-dip lurch, and I ran toward him. An aquarium guard hollered and ran toward the fisherman from the opposite side. We reached him at the same moment, stopping the fishing expedition. Donnie looked up at me and calmly stated, "I told you I was going to go fishing here."

The guard kept the fishing line, and I assured him I'd keep my student next to me during our visit. Donnie was right. He had told me he was going to fish on our field trip. He'd been perfectly honest, and I'd been just plain stupid to think my answer about only looking and learning would be enough to squelch the plan. Luckily, we'd caught him before he'd hauled in any fish.

Donnie stayed near me for the entire visit at my bidding. If he strayed even a bit, I held his hand—mortifying to a fourth grader. I breathed a sigh of relief as we left the aquarium to eat lunch and board the boats. Silly me.

Mr. Fisherman tried again on the boat ride. I spent my time counting heads off and on. On about the third count, one head suddenly turned into a small behind instead. There was my boy, leaning over the far side of the boat, another string and hook dangling into Lake Michigan. Why hadn't I checked his pockets?

I lunged and grabbed the waist of his shorts and hauled him back onto the seat. "I told you..." He got no farther as I hissed at him. "Don't say it!"

This time, I searched all his pockets. No more fishing lines, but the darned kid smirked at me all the way home. He'd warned me multiple times and he'd still carried out his plan. It stinks when a little kid wins out over a grown woman.

Much later, when I didn't have to worry about being tossed out of the Shedd Aquarium or losing a child overboard on a boat, I laughed about the way Donnie had fooled me. Oddly enough, we established a bond that day and he proved to be a model student for the rest of the school year. Teachers regularly charge their students to listen. After my experience with the would-be fisherman, I learned that I also needed to listen more carefully to my students.

-Nancy Julien Kopp

Flying, Crashing Children!

"CAN I MAKE PETER fly?" I asked the director of the play.

"Do you think you can do that?" He asked in return.

"Well, I think so," I said, as calm as possible, while inwardly, my brain screamed JACKPOT! I was going to make Peter Pan fly!

It was spring in Abqaiq, Saudi Arabia, time for the annual Middle School theatrical production and a highlight of the year for students and parents. They had recruited me to help build the sets. Now I also had the daunting task of propelling children airborne without maiming them.

Knowing my technical shortcomings, I immediately strode down the hall to recruit an industrial arts teacher, Dan. A friend with the technical skills to help me put this plan in motion. Together, we had to figure out how to make Peter, Wendy, John, and Michael fly around the stage in three scenes. In the opening scene alone, we would have to put all the kids in the air at the same time.

Dan and I set to work in the next few days, drawing up some initial plans and working out some rudimentary ideas. We decided on two flying methods after initial trial and error with props. The boys and Wendy would only have to fly around the bedroom. We would attach them to static cables to leap off of beds and dressers, hurtling out and back as if on a rope swing. Peter's flying would be a somewhat more complicated matter. We wanted him to fly up and down, back and forth, and side to side.

Dan and I settled on using two cables. A static one that I would control to raise or lower the seventh-grade child. Dan would handle the second cable, enabling him to pull Peter backward and up, lifting thirty feet to the top of the stage. We thought the concept was sound. The plan was for the lucky girl chosen to play Peter to fly out of the clouds from up in the rafters through the bedroom window, land, jump up again, and fly around the room.

To make it work, Peter would have to be lying on her stomach behind the window frame on the stage. When on the proper cue, Dan, from behind the set, would jump down from a bench, pulling his cable to the floor. This would lift Peter up and backward into the rafters. Meanwhile, I would control the static line on a little foot grip ramp to raise or lower her on cue.

What could go wrong?

We tested the device several times with props before strapping her into it. Her father inspected the device and agreed it seemed safe. After several practice sessions, we had Peter flying about with confidence. The other kids flew off their designated perches and returned for soft landings.

The poor eighth-grade girl playing Wendy Darling did not fare well during our third rehearsal. We attached the cable to her waist a bit too low. When we jerked her up, she flipped over from the waist, sweeping the floor with her hair, before spinning around like a top. Following a brief moment of terror, the entire cast had a good laugh. However, watching the poor girl revolve helplessly should have been a harbinger of future things.

For the dress rehearsal, our director sent brochures to the surrounding schools, and soon word quickly spread that "kids will fly!" Dan and I thought we had worked out the kinks and were eager to launch the children. On the day of the show, the theater was packed with students and parents, and the audience was virtually humming in anticipation.

As the curtain rose, I couldn't help but notice Peter's father, sitting third-row center with a nervous smile. As the first flying scene approached, I glanced at our star lying belly down on the stage behind the window set. She flashed me a beaming smile with a confident thumb up, signaling that she was ready to fly.

At least she's ready, I thought, holding my breath, a firm grip on my cable handle as I dug my feet in. I could not see Dan behind the large set at the rear of the stage, who, like me, waited for the musical cue to set the whole shebang in motion. I tried to picture the crowd's reaction when we launched Peter. Would they cheer, create thunderous applause, or sit in astonished silence? Suddenly, the music announced our cue. Snapping out of my brief reverie, I pulled back slowly to time my lift as the lights faded. I could hear the thump of Dan jumping from his bench and then watched the young actress lift to her thirty-foot height up in the raters. At the moment she reached her peak, I heard Dan call out. "Oh No!"

Oh no? Oh no, what? That's not good.

The clip attached to the back of Peter's vest ring snapped. Attached only to my cable, nothing more than a swinging pendulum, Peter flipped upside down, just as Wendy had done. She began to fly down and forward from the thirty feet above the hardwood stage. I pulled with all my strength and dug my feet to keep her from dropping full force on her head. I had no idea how much slack to give her to allow her to "fly" down. It must have seemed spectacular to the audience, who had no idea what was happening. Here came Peter, zooming out of a dark sky through the lit bedroom window. I pedaled backward as hard as possible as Peter, arms outstretched, flew outward and upward, past the stage and over the gasping crowd, before reversing into a screeching halt. Our star made a graceful, pinpoint stop on the last inch of the stage. She rocked back and forth on her tiptoes, arms waving frantically, the audience holding its collective breath until, as she finally settled, they broke into a raucous cheer.

Her father, in whose lap she almost landed, gripped the arms of his seat as if being electrocuted. He peeled his wife's fingers out of his arm before smiling, more from relief than appreciation. I could sense from his shaking head that he would probably have a word or two with the morons who nearly launched his daughter into the nickel seats.

Catching my breath, I stifled a laugh when I heard Dan's voice filter through the wall.

"Is she alive?"

I realized he was blind behind the set, having no idea what had happened.

During Act Two, the actors playing Wendy's brothers were over-excited about being "live on stage." Soaring too fast, they spun, arms and legs akimbo, wildly around in the air before missing their landing marks, repeatedly slamming back into the set walls. Dan and I braced the walls from the back as the boys smashed into the walls on each return. The boys were having a grand time, as we could hear them laughing and shrieking through the walls. The crowd thought this hilarious as they egged the rascals on. These human-wrecking balls spun around above the stage, probably hoping that they would bring the whole set down.

Ultimately, Dan and I could only claim that the sets we built remained in one piece and not one child received injuries. However, we turned Peter Pan, a poignant tale of childhood, into a slapstick comedy.

But in the end, Peter Pan did indeed fly. The following year, the larger Dharan School north of us put on the same play. Peter Pan flapped his arms and walked onstage. The audience was not impressed.

-Kevin Baxter

THAT WASN'T IN THE JOB DESCRIPTION...

I believe the term is "Working Remotely" not "Remotely Working" dear

The Rainy-Day Job Interview

S O, PICTURE THIS, RIGHT? It's seven in the morning and I am NOT a morning person. The sun was barely visible, and I already had an 8 a.m. appointment looming over me. A job interview. So, yes, I was off to a rocky start. Did I mention it was raining—the kind of rain that has ducks applying for life insurance.

Now, don't get me wrong, I love rain. It's nature's free pass for being lazy, no yard work, and you can enjoy refreshing air curled up with a favorite book and pot of tea.

As I stepped out of my car at the downtown parking lot, I looked like a million bucks in my best suit, hair, and makeup, all ready to wow them. But within a few seconds, my curly hair took a trip back to the 80s, tripling in size. My makeup turned into a Picasso painting, and my expensive umbrella gave me a gymnastic show, flipping inside out.

"Now's not the time, Umbrella!" I shouted as I battled to control the rebellious piece of rain protection. In all the chaos, my left shoe decided to play hide-and-seek and slipped off, darting under my car.

"Really?"

Struggling to balance on one foot and armed with a twisted umbrella, I tried my best to rescue my shoe. It was an epic failure. The shoe stayed put. I stood on one foot, my tights soaked, drenched like a flamingo.

Desperate, I moved my car. My visibility was so poor, that I could barely see the bright red hue of my tiny Volkswagen bug. And guess what? I backed into a low cement bank. It was just a tap, but it was like a kick for my bug, causing the bumper to droop half off.

"Blast it!" I yelled at the rain-soaked world. But I could finally see my shoe! Snatching it up and cramming my wet foot back in, I moved the car and dashed for the interview building.

To add a cherry on top of this disaster sundae, guess what? The boss canceled the interview because of the storm! "Who would be crazy enough to drive in this?" his administrative assistant said. Well, apparently, me.

Squishing my way back to the car, I used my sopping wet tights to fasten the hanging bumper back up and drove home laughing. You know that saying, "If you want to make God laugh, tell him about your plans?" That day, I think I had the big guy in stitches.

Ironically, it turns out this soggy disaster wasn't in vain. Despite my no-show interview boss, I got the job! My new boss admired my dedication to show up despite the storm. And get this, I get to work from home! So, no more early mornings, no need to brave the weather, and no yard work. Instead, I can afford a lawn service now! So, there you go. Sometimes, even the worst days can be the best, in a slapstick comedy kind of way.

-A. C. Blake

Holy Grail

T HE BOOKSTORE WHERE I worked was unusually packed that one afternoon. All of us were busy jostling around assisting customers and arranging books that were left cluttered about by the coffee lounge. I was about to take my lunch break when *he came* in. He swaggered around like he owned the place, chatting loudly with his entourage of young men who seemed more like his peons than friends. When I looked at who was disturbing the crowded sales floor, I realized it was some hotshot TV star who happened to be one of the lead actors in an afternoon soap opera.

He paraded around with his entourage in tow, demanding a sales clerk to talk to. My co-workers warned me of his attitude, but they still pushed me up front, saying I should feel lucky to help an actor like him. I smiled at them wryly, put up my friendly sales face, and asked politely how I could help. The actor commanded I find him a book. After he gave me the author's name, I ran it through the inventory system. It turned out there was one copy left. The problem was, no matter how hard we searched, it wasn't on the sales floor. The actor's voice strained with impatience as the floor manager negotiated with him. I was lucky enough to be elected, *again*, to go down to the basement storeroom to find it.

The storeroom was a labyrinth of books piled high. I navigated my way, carefully noting every label from subject to surname, but still, I couldn't find it. I must have been there a while when my co-workers burst in, frantically asking if I found it. The actor was making a scene, furious that it was taking me that long to find the book. The floor manager told them to come help search the place.

It was the most painstaking excavation I ever experienced. We pried every pile, careful not to topple anything down or spend the entire night re-arranging them. Then, *finally*, I found it. Lodged between the non-fiction books and the children's encyclopedia pile, just lying there on the floor in the darkest corner. It was big and hardbound, with a lousy-looking cover. Anyone not paying much attention might easily mistake it for an encyclopedia. No wonder it took us a long time to find it. I wiped my sweaty palms and picked it up with utmost care, raising it against the light and smiling. When the others noticed what I held, they pushed me up the elevator, I was told to go immediately to our most valued customer of the day and give it to him.

He was still standing by the cashier counter, flirting with the sales ladies. His entourage flocked back near him when they saw me coming with the book. The actor snobbishly smiled, stretched out his hand, and took the book. He examined it as his entourage crowded behind him. His smile widened as he looked at the back inner flap jacket and said, "See? I told you I looked exactly like him."

I was so dumbstruck by his remark that I fell completely silent. He shoved back the book at my chest, told me I did a good job, and strolled off out the door with his entourage.

One of my co-workers found me still standing there, all quiet, looking at the door where the actor left. When he asked me how it went, I just said the dumbest thing.

"He said he looked like the author," I said to him.

"He looked just like the author."

I shoved the book at my co-worker and told him to keep it back where we found it. Some place dark, where it could easily get lost.

-Bien Santillan Mabbayad

I'm No Evel Knievel- *Confessions of a Recovering Actor in Hollywood*

E VEL KNIEVEL, THE LEGENDARY, daredevil stuntman of the 70's, broke numerous records and hundreds of bones. People did not want to see him die. They wanted to see him defy death. Full disclosure...I'm no Evel Knievel. If you want to see me defy death, you're welcome to join me every morning and watch me wake up in my warm comfy bed to the sound of my radio alarm. Take that, Grim Reaper...Victory is mine.

I remember, when I was a kid, I used to go to the amusement park to drive those bumper cars. The objective was to crash into as many cars as possible while trying not to get hit yourself. I guess that was supposed to be fun. Not for me. For me, the object was simply to avoid being hit at all costs. While the other kids were out there whooping and hollering and slamming into each other, I was playing it safe. At the age of 8, I was already a defensive driver. Hey, if they had turning signals on those bumper cars, I would have used them.

They say real men don't eat quiche. I eat quiche...and kale, and enjoy afternoon tea with assorted finger sandwiches and warm scones with clotted cream. I have no need to prove that I am a real man. The fact of the matter is, men used to frighten me. There was always a feeling of domination and rivalry. Men were like a troop of chimps patrolling their territory. It was a blood sport and everyone was in it to win. I was not up for the challenge. There can only be one Alpha male. My strategy...Just stay out of everyone's way. So, 'no', I was never one of the boys.

What I am, is a recovering actor. As it turns out, acting is a contact sport. If you want to find work, it helps to know somebody. I happened to meet another dad at my kid's pre-school who was in the biz.

He said to me, "I understand you're an actor.

"Yeah", I said.

"Great, I'll put you to work. I'm directing this Thursday. I'll call you."

"What? Wait. Don't you want me to audition?"

"Nah. Nobody reads for me."

"Okay, Great".

Of course, like so many other Hollywood stories, I figured I'd never hear from him. Wednesday night, my phone rings. It's him. "Be on set at 6 a.m."

I showed up early the next morning. I was the first to arrive. Little by little the rest of the actors showed up. All men. Some were buff. Some were huge. Some were thin and wiry. Some had potbellies. Some were hung over. They all seemed to know each other. I felt completely out of place: A total outsider in the company of men. Finally, my contact showed up. It turns out, he was what they call the second unit director. I really didn't know what that was. He immediately did a head count and broke us up into two teams; "Good Guys" and "Bad Guys". He looked at me for a second, but did not yet put me on either team. Like me, he was not sure where I belonged. He then started doling out assignments. "You're rolling the car. You're doing the burn. You're doing the fall." Then it hit me; this guy's the stunt coordinator! What have I gotten myself into? Does he assume *all* men want to jump off of a five-story building? Sorry, it turns out, not all men are created equal. Suddenly, I *am* Evel Knievel.

Contrary to popular belief, there is almost no training and very few safety precautions for doing stunt work. It is simply risky and dangerous. And this is where I got to re-think my opinion of men. I was able to see them as their best selves. Like those territorial chimps, they became a band of brothers. They had each other's backs. They were all in this together. A good day for a stunt team is when everyone gets to go home safe and sound. As for me, up to that point, the only contribution I had made to the stunt team was explaining to them what ratatouille was when lunch was served.

Motorcycle crashes. Car chases. Explosions. Gunfire. After witnessing these stunt guys risking life and limb all day long, I wondered if I'd actually get the chance to do anything.

Then, sometime after midnight, my friend came up to me and said, "All right, you're driving the getaway car."

"What? Wait!" Panicked, I said, "But, but..."

He said, "Don't worry. It's nothing. You're going to have a walkie-talkie in the car with you. All you have to do is; when I say 'roll camera', you start the car rolling. When I say 'action', you hit it! Go as fast as you can. When you come to the stop sign, I want you to blow through it. Don't worry; I'll have the police holding traffic...Make a left. If you can screech the tires, great...and make sure you hit your mark, because I'll have a camera tracking you. Got it?"

"Got it!" Truth be told, the last thing I remembered hearing was, "You're driving the getaway car." Sitting there, waiting for direction, my heart was racing faster than the car engine. And then, "Roll camera". I began to roll. The director yelled, 'Action'. I hit it! I was off and running. I was flying. I blew through the stop sign. I made the left. The tires were screeching. Flying down the next street, I hit my mark!

"And cut!"

Done! I did it! Exhilarated and feeling like one of the boys and looking for a little praise and acknowledgment, I got on the walkie to check in with the director.... I said, "So how was that?"

To which he responded, "It was all right, but we have to go again."

"What?!?... Why?!?"

He said, "Bad guys don't use turning signals."

Quiche, anyone?

-Gary Koppel

Meow

MAY I SAY, SOME days working for an animal shelter may not be any different than working for the zoo. The roars are replaced with meows and there are several creatures available for display. I am one of three individuals who answer the phone for the shelter. The questions that I receive throughout the day include "Do you have any Yorkies?" or "Can animal control come pick up this opossum?"

One Friday, I heard the phone ring. I went ahead and answered waiting to see where *this* call would take me. On the other line, I heard a gentleman say, "Hey I saw smoke while driving past your shelter, is everything ok?"

"Yes sir, everything is fine. We have a vet clinic being built next door, so the wielders are probably being a bit overzealous."

There was a brief pause before a small chuckle erupted and the caller stated, "Well, I'm glad to hear that. I didn't want to just drive past without saying anything."

I thanked him and placed the phone back down on the receiver. Turning to my coworker to tell her about my interaction, I saw smoke bellowing down the street. From the far left a great wall of smoke erupted from the rear of the shelter. My eyes met with my coworker who mouthed call 911.

My fingers quickly dialed 911 as dark smoke gathered towards the front door. The operator asked me three times for my location. I eventually said, "The place where Sarah McLachlan loves to visit with animals crying in the background." Several minutes later a firetruck finally arrived to investigate the scene. We assumed that one of the construction workers accidentally set fire to some of their equipment. Or potentially the auto shop nearby was the true culprit.

It was the dumpster.

Our dumpster was on fire. The shelter was a literal dumpster fire.

A firefighter walked into the front lobby and threw inside a truck tire that had been slightly seared and melted. What popped out of the inner lining was a white domestic short-haired cat with a stomach the size of a watermelon.

After a ten-day stray hold, there I was placing a promo online for someone to adopt Dumpster Fire, a spayed female white cat with an unforgettable origin story.

-Karl Stevenson

Working Post Retirement-Are We Having Fun Yet?

H IS NAME WAS CHICKLETS, and he was the manager on my shift. Ok, that wasn't his real name – it's Vince, but no one called him that. I made the mistake of calling him Vince the first day I worked and he threw a taco shell at me. Hard, not soft.

I am retired. I taught language arts to special needs kids in Arizona for 39 years. When people hear that, they express awe and say something like, 'you must be a very patient person.' Here's the truth: I'm as patient as a 68-year-old with a weak bladder stuck on the I-5 in Los Angeles at 5 o'clock on Friday afternoon. And yes, that did happen to me. Point is, I'm not particularly patient. Teaching, for me, was easy and fun.

The exact opposite of my post-retirement job.

I didn't need to work. But my wife firmly suggested that I find something to keep me busy. I tried gardening, but all my greenery turned brown. Then, because I had a grandfather who was a master baker, I tried my hand at baking. After permanently disabling my wife's Mixmaster, she *permanently* evicted me from the kitchen. So much for genetics.

As a result, I decided to try my hand at something that was not in close proximity to my wife.

Which is probably what she had in mind all along.

I picked the job because I like tacos. I naively believed that because I liked something so much, preparing them for someone else would be a piece of cake, excuse the metaphor. Well, that and the fact that they would hire a 68-year-old with no fast-food experience on the spot.

My title was Team Member, which sounds a whole lot like someone you'd find at Disneyland, pedaling Dole Whip or running the Teacups.

My first day went something like this: work faster, refried beans do not go on the cinnabons, refried beans *do* go on the bean burritos, work faster, hard tacos do not have soft shells, that's too much ice in the drinks, soft tacos do not have hard shells, you're working too slow, put more ice in the drinks.

A boost to my self-esteem it was not.

I was surprised on my second day for two reasons. First, I had a second day, and even better, they assigned me to the drive-through. Good for me. I couldn't possibly mess this up.

I was wrong.

Imagine for a moment trying to communicate to someone on your roof, through the chimney, as your wife is running the vacuum cleaner.

That I got any of the orders correct was a matter of sheer luck. But when I neglected to 'hold the cheese' for someone who was lactose intolerant, I crossed the fast-food Rubicon.

I was fired.

My wife, typically my surefire support system, thought it was the funniest thing she had ever heard. She couldn't wait to regale our extended family with my outrageous screw-up. However, when I informed said wife that I was thinking about starting a blog, whereby I could work from home, her mirthfulness quickly dissipated.

"What's a blob?"

"It's called a blog. I'm going to call it Crabazon. People can post their negative experiences with buying things online; like having the wrong thing delivered, having it delivered broken, or with missing pieces. It should be very popular."

"Why don't you just try something you're already good at?"

"What am I good at?" I innocently posed.

"You're pretty good with kids, as I recall."

Which led to my second post-retirement job and one which I have managed not to get fired from for six weeks.

I am the four-hour noon-duty aide at an elementary school three blocks from my house. I help with lunch for the kindergarteners, then conduct sports activities with the 4th, 5th, and 6th graders.

And I'm having a ball. There is simply nothing more gratifying than to walk into a school cafeteria and have a bevy of five and six-year-olds cry out, "Hi, Mr. Dave!"

If there's a lesson to be learned from this experience, it's an obvious one: pick something you like AND you're good at. And if you do accept a job at a fast-food restaurant that serves tacos, learn to duck. Take it from me- those hard-shell tacos can leave a mark.

-Dave Bachmann

Vintage Hospitality

I WAS ONCE VICE-PRESIDENT (Asia-Pacific) for an American charity that recruited me after I retired as a not-for-profit CEO in Australia. At that time, I visited many Asian countries and never ceased to delight in the people I met and their cultures. As an aging white Anglo-Saxon man, I have no doubt that there were times when the people I met were less than delighted with my cultural faux pas on my learning journey but they were unfailingly gracious.

I was once in Seoul, meeting with a potential South Korean supplier. We were in an old part of the city in a building which is part office and part museum. We had all removed our shoes. While we talked, we partook of seemingly endless cups of tea prepared and drunk in the traditional manner. Some of these teas have been preserved for decades and are discussed with all the seriousness of vintage wines in our culture.

It was mutually understood that no decisions would be made today or even at any time in the near future, as is the norm in most Asian cultures. Eventually, it came time to leave. I sat on what I perceived to be a solid-looking stool to put my shoes back on. Something indefinable shifted in the mood, although the smiles remained.

Walking down the laneway leading away from the building, I took our interpreter discreetly aside and tested whether I have sensed the mood correctly. He politely informed me that the 'stool' I sat on was a 400-year-old ceremonial tea table and only its superior craftmanship had averted disaster for all concerned.

-Doug Jacquier

Puddles and Power Outages

WORK WAS CURSED. TERRIBLE. A complete and utter disaster. I won't say that it was the absolute worst because there can always be worse days, but it was a *nightmare*.

When I got to work, there was a massive puddle on the counter-something was leaking. Eventually, it got cleaned up but we had to shut off the water to fix it, which made for a lot of unhappy customers. (Although, should I call them customers if all they get is *free* ice and water?)

It took two hours for the maintenance guy to even show up. Not his fault, but still. After figuring out how to fix it, the guy left to get some tools-and a new part of the machine started leaking. This one came with a loud buzzing noise that made me wish my ears were detachable! Finally, they got it settled-not quite back to 100 percent, but operational.

Things were actually going well for an hour or two when the power shut down for a few seconds. And even after the electricity whirred back on, the register decided it didn't want to let me back into the session. We finally got it working again when a second power outage slammed into the store. This time the lights stayed off for good. I stood there in the dark, just waiting. The ice cream was sure to melt if the blackout continued, but there wasn't anything I could do about that. Soon enough, my manager came up to me and told me to count the till-we had to shut down early because of the outage. I quickly counted out the till and dragged my weary feet out the door.

But like I said before, there can always be worse days. I mean, I know someone had an even worse day than I did: turns out a drunk driver had swerved into one of the power poles and an entire portion of town went dark. I'll stick to my nightmare instead.

-K.J. Carter

Snow, Cold, and the Heat Tape

After completing graduate school, my wife, Mikayla, and I moved to a small town in Northern Vermont with our 2-year-old daughter, Maryanne. I would start my career teaching at a local community college. We bought a 12x60 mobile home, and our life in the North Country began. The trailer park manager visited while we were moving in. He gave us a list of rules with two warnings. "Ya' gotta put sealer on ya' roof. Melting snow will seep int' the seams and leak into ya' home. My nephew Ralphy will put sealer on ya' roof. He does good work and don't charge much. His phone number is at the bottom of the list of rules. Finally, ya' got t' know about th' heat tape. Follow me."

We followed him to the back, where an electric cord from under the mobile home plugged into an electrical outlet. A plastic bubble, with a small bulb inside, was at the plug-end of the cord. He explained how the heat tape wraps around the pipe that comes from the well. If the bulb is out, we are in trouble because that means the tape isn't keeping the pipe warm, freezing the pipe—trouble, toilet trouble! He continued, "Heat tapes usually stop working at night in the Winter. So, when ya' go out to put on a new heat tape, be sure t' have ya' shotgun with ya'. If you go out at night 'ya might see a bear. Don't try t' play with it. Bears like to eat people. One last thing. Ya' gotta put on a skirt 'round ya' home. Ralphy does good work, don't charge much. He builds skirts with a door for ya' t' get at a burned-out heat tape. That's it. Bye folks," he said and left.

The picture he painted *terrified* me. The heat tape usually stops working at night. Wonderful. Bears might want to keep me company. *Why didn't I apply for a job in Florida?* It's too late now.

The next day, Sunday, after breakfast, I put on my coat and boots and went out to check the heat tape. It was on. My wife reminded me I had checked the heat tape before breakfast. She didn't understand that checking the heat tape was going to be a ritual for me if I was going to maintain my sanity. Fear is a great motivator. Before lunch, it was ritual time. I looked at the outdoor thermometer and cringed. The temperature was 15 F (-9 C). I assumed that by the time I went out to check the heat tape, the temperature would be 100 degrees below zero. Fortunately, I was wrong. I returned with the news that it was snowing but told Mikayla it would just be a dusting. While we were eating lunch, she opened the door and exclaimed that the duster was becoming a blizzard. Unfortunately, I was wrong. In fact, the mother of all winters was on its way.

The next morning, I went to the kitchen and looked out the window. I called to Mikayla to come to the kitchen. She came, and we looked outside, exclaiming to unnamed deities that we were good people and didn't deserve to suffer. The car and the steps were both under a million feet of snow. How would I get to the college? I turned on the radio to see if I could get a weather report. "...the sale ends this weekend. Now, to the weather. Everything's closed. Have a good day."

The next morning, Mikayla dressed Maryanne and went outside while I checked the heat tape. It was working. I sat on the couch and read. As I read, drops of water fell on my book. I looked up. "Oh, my Gosh," I gasped. I rushed from one room to another. "In one hour, this place is going to be a mobile swimming pool."

There was a knock at the door, and I rushed to open it. It was Ralphy. He charged me $20 to shovel the snow off the roof. That was a lot of money in 1967, but it was worth it because it stopped raining inside. Ralphy also charged me $60 to put the sealer that I should have put on when we moved in. Live and learn.

At last, Christmas came, and we went home for the holidays. The only problem with going home was having to come back to tons of snow, the unbelievable cold, and heat tape. We got back around 9:00 p.m. on a Sunday. I unpacked the car and Mikayla took Maryanne to the bathroom. As I unpacked, Mikayla screamed. I rushed in. "What's wrong?"

"The toilet overflowed. The water pipe must be frozen."

I gasped and rushed out, immediately returning. "Guess who's heat tape burned out?" I grabbed a heat tape and a flashlight from our junk drawer, took a shovel from the car, and plodded through a million feet of snow to the heat tape...at 9:30 at night. "Bears don't run around at night in the winter, do they? They hibernate in the winter, don't they?" I mumbled as I shoveled snow away from the skirt door. Once in, I unplugged the burned-out heat tape, but to unwrap it from the water pipe, I had to dig through another tundra. After two hours of torture, I could *finally* unwrap it, followed by wrapping the new heat tape around the pipe. I backed out, closed the door, and plugged in the new heat tape. Shivering convulsively, I went back into the house and Mikayla helped me take off my frozen jacket. "Mikayla, I can't... feel... anything,"

"I know, Josh," she replied sympathetically. "I'll fill the tub with warm water. There should be some warm water left in the water heater."

By morning, the water pipe had thawed. While we ate breakfast, I lost it. "How can anybody live like this? As long as it's a million degrees below zero out there, that heat tape could blow. I don't sleep anymore. I lie awake listening to the heat tape, and that's bad, because the heat tape doesn't make any noise. What do the poor, homeless people do? Just freeze to death?"

"Josh, all the poor, homeless people from here move to Florida for the winter."

Well, winter finally ended, the semester ended, and we agreed that we endured enough of the snow, cold, and heat tape. After I submitted my resignation, we packed a U-Haul truck. Mikayla drove the car and I drove the truck. At last, we were going home.

-Saul Greenblatt

Scarring Day

H AVING ONLY THREE PEOPLE scheduled for Food Stamp Day was the worst. Our manager really should've known better, but she only scheduled two people to be cashiers and one person for food. Food Stamp Day is so busy that the line wraps around the store as people wait for their turn to use the three kiosks.

On this particular summery day, the weather was a perfect sunny afternoon. There were many people ordering food, but there was only one of me.

Corporate had made the decision to get rid of our food-grade can opener because apparently, it cost too much to replace. We had this cheap can opener instead. So, when I ran out of black olives, I needed to open a new can. When I proceeded to do so, it swung backward, cutting my hand open. (I still have a scar from it.)

Of course, none of the customers had a clue what was going on. I'm freaking out because I could see "inside" my hand. I ran to the back and washed out the wound, not knowing what exactly I was supposed to do.

One of my coworkers saw my hand bleeding. She was freaking out —which only fueled my anxiety to be even worse than what it was.

The second one came over and wrapped my hand up for the night until after work because they couldn't get anyone to answer their phones or come in so I could go to the emergency room. So, I headed back out. All the customers were staring me down; none of them understood in the least.

One customer said something smart to me and I countered: "Sorry, I cut my hand open." That seemed to shut him up.

Then after work, we headed to the emergency room. It took them an hour before they would look at me even though I was the only one there. Fortunately, my friend waited for me and gave me a ride home after the emergency room visit where I had to get a tetanus shot, my hand was glued shut, and they gave me butterfly stitches.

Customer service definitely isn't for the weak.

-Linda M. Crate

Lost in Transit

I N THE EARLY 2000S, mobile phones were still relatively uncommon. However, I'm not sure if having a cell phone would have helped anything.

In a small town in Ireland (Europe), where I lived, finding a good job was like finding a needle in a haystack. Just graduated, I wanted to move out of my parent's house. My heart almost stopped beating when I saw an ad in the newspaper for a job in a nearby city. I called the company right away and scheduled an interview.

On the day of the interview, it had been raining since morning. My last wish was to arrive at the destination completely soaked. Neither my parents nor I had a car. To get to the city, which was about 62 miles (100 km) away, I had to take the train. Actually, two: there were no direct connections between my town and the city. Therefore, I planned my trip with a transfer. The interview was scheduled for early afternoon, so I had plenty of time to get there.

At least, I thought. And then, when I got off the first train, I realized I'd lost my wallet.

Was it stolen? It was devastating to lose my bank card, ID, and my money. Fortunately, I still had some loose cash in my bag.

Since I had only a short time before my next train connection, I tried calling my bank from a phone booth. The wait time on the helpline was unbearable, and when someone finally answered, the authentication process took forever. I was told that I needed to report the loss to the police right away.

I still had almost 30 minutes before the next train left, and the police station was at the train station. I went there to resolve my issue. Everything took longer than expected, and by the time I left the police station, my train was already waiting on the platform.

I got on the train at the last minute and found a seat quickly. I took out my materials again to prepare for the interview. About 30 minutes later, I started getting ready to get off at my destination, but the train was still moving fast. I looked out the window and didn't recognize any of the sights we passed. *Maybe it is still raining?* After another 10 minutes of travel, I asked another passenger when we'd arrive. When he mentioned a different city than the one I was going to, I was gobsmacked. "The train is going the other way," he said when I explained where I wanted to go. "Our next stop is almost 62 miles away."

I felt desperate at that moment. I was on the wrong train. Even though I had some money left, I couldn't get to my bank account. I couldn't get in touch with the company where I had the interview. There was no way I could call my parents. To top it off, the rain intensified, making me even more angry.

Once we got to the station, my first thought was to call the company and reschedule the interview. They didn't answer their phone, though. In my head, I was going to call them first thing in the morning. There was only one thing left to do: find out the train's return time. But I was in for a diabolic surprise when finding out the next train wasn't until the next morning.

The hotel I found near the station was definitely too expensive for my means. And they didn't offer any discount for a soaked, desperate-looking young man without ID. I was hungry, defeated, penniless, and doomed to spend the night at the station. Clenching my teeth, I thought I'd make it through. A little more than an hour later, the cashier told me that the station would be closed for the night. Seeing my condition, she advised me to ask the priest for shelter at the nearby church.

That's what I did. The priest was an elderly man who acted more like a soldier than a spiritual being. Skeptical at first, he eventually let me stay the night. My bed was in a damp, small room with a peculiar smell. I couldn't sleep despite my exhaustion, and I heard the priest moving around the house late into the night. Maybe he was worried I'd steal something...

The following morning, I contacted my parents. When my dad heard what I went through, he rented a car from a neighbor and picked me up. I begged him to go with me to the company office. A padlock on the entrance and an empty office greeted us when we got there. Then a woman working next door told us the police had come the day before. She saw handcuffed company representatives being led out, but didn't know the details. (I later found out the company's CEO was accused of tax fraud). As we drove home, we remained in complete silence, unsure whether to laugh or cry.

-M.M. Stansky

Not the Time or Place

I DREW THE SHORT straw and ended up leaning on the ency-clopedia case in the reference section collecting raffle tickets, right outside the glass doors of the rare book room where the annual Holiday Gathering was coalescing. As each of the mostly elderly Friends of the Library entered, I handed them a small slip of paper and pencil, repeating directions: "You have to write your name. On the slip of paper. The slip of paper. Yes, that's right."

Shifting from foot to foot, staring into space, a bad idea crept into my consciousness. *Perhaps writing some fun words on the raffle tickets would relieve my intense boredom?*

In prior years, there was just one raffle winner, so what were the chances of my fake names getting called? Zero. Zilch. *Hohoho*, I scribbled, smiling, feeling brave. *Falalalalala* I wrote next, those first silly words loosening something tight inside me. Recklessly, a little hysterically, I started a series of names: *Mike Rowave. Mag Azine. Jim Nasium.* I allowed a small, insane giggle to escape my lips. I added another *hohoho* just to seal the deal.

Any good reference librarian would have asked the pertinent questions. *What are you hoping to achieve by this? Is this actually funny? Is this respectful to the Friends of the Library? What will you do if one of your fake names gets called? How do you know for sure there is only one prize?* Oh, that last question was one I should have pondered. But that end of the workday malaise, the presence of the very old ticking grandfather clock peering over my shoulder, and the musty smell of books taunted, *Write another phony name, who cares?*

As it turned out, there were *five* prizes that year. When I ap-proached my colleague, the tech guru who was in charge, to re-scind my erroneous entries, her expression contorted. Her hold on the ticket bowl stiffened. We began this back-and-forth thing that went on a touch too long.

"What is your problem?" she asked, yanking one last time.

I let go, realizing I needed to stand back and watch how this thing was going to play out. Sweating slightly, I gnawed on a piece of candied grapefruit peel, bitter stuff we made fun of every year. I took my penance orally and leaned against the back display case, the one holding part of the *Dead Sea Scrolls* or something.

It was the old art librarian, wearing a mid-length black dress and pearls, an alumna and thirty-plus year employee, who threw her hand in the bowl to pick the first name. I held my breath as she swished around. I repeated a newly formed mantra: *There is no way. No way. There is no WAY.* The intrusive grandfather clock ticked off the seconds. I sipped my punch, the sweet ginger-ale taste lingering in the back of my mouth. When her face screwed up in annoyance, I knew. *I knew.* She looked at the tech lady and said bitterly, "*Someone. Is. Trying. To. Be. Smart.*" Her hand crumpled the raffle ticket in, if not anger, deep annoyance. I looked around. The Friends of the Library shrugged, looking around themselves. Some didn't hear. One man, head back, snored in a deep snooze.

Then, my extremely elegant boss, the head of public services, took over, sliding her well-manicured hand into the bowl. Would she sit me down and lecture me after this? I deserved it, for sure. She landed on a ticket, removed it, and unfolded it. She then said, with her best annunciation, *Mike Ro-Wahv,* fancily pronouncing my joke name. No one flinched. She called it again. I shrunk, realizing how I should have told someone, just to have an ally, but it was too late, impossible. It was that day I learned that having a joke by yourself isn't fun, not at all. The pain continued, like plantar fasciitis or a throbbing sciatic nerve. She shook her head and reached in again. "Jim Nahsium?" calling the over-pronounced version of the name. She called out several times, looking for this Jim Nahsium fellow in the crowd. *How could Mike and Jim not be here after entering the raffle?* No one caught on. Nonplussed, she laughed slightly and returned her hand to the bowl for another name. Finally I shot forward, unable to withstand anymore.

"Those. Those were joke names. I put them in! Mike Rowave. Get it? Microwave. And Jim Nasium, like gymnasium?"

It all sounded so stupid, so infantile. One lady's mouth dropped in horror. Others laughed uncomfortably. My face heated, beaded in sweat. The sweets I'd imbibed earlier curdled in my tightening throat.

"Well," the tech lady said, "You will NOT receive your pack of greeting cards!"

My punishment, more embarrassing, more ridiculous than the crime.

-Maggie Nerz Iribarne

THAT WENT WELL...

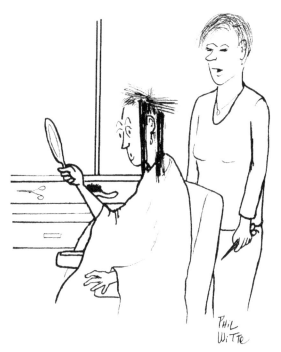

Expect smaller aftershocks in the coming days!

Beep! Beep! BEEP!

S TARTLED, I SHOT UP from a dead sleep and blearily looked around my cramped college dorm room. The floor, littered with clothes, and the desk, crowded with overpriced textbooks, were barely visible as dusty sunlight weakly peeked through the blinds. Grumbling, I rubbed my eyes and reached for my phone. A quick glance at the clock confirmed my fear.

It was 6:00 AM.

On a Saturday.

And I was wide awake.

After struggling with the blankets tangled around my legs, I descended to the floor with all the grace and agility of a dizzy elephant. Slightly more awake now, I tried to find the source of that deafening screech that had woken me up several hours earlier than anyone would ever want.

Had the Purge descended upon my school?

Was my neighbor blaring death metal rock?

Did a lab experiment go terribly wrong and now the CIA was moving to quarantine all the students?

Yawning, I realized I was wrong on all three accounts. That horrible, soul-crushing, ear-splitting sound tormenting my ears like nails on a chalkboard could only be one thing.

The fire alarm.

Discontentedly muttering, I wrapped my blanket tight around my shoulders and headed for the door. In my half-asleep state, I forgot in the case of fires, you are supposed to save yourself, leaving behind your personal belongings. I snagged my computer on the way out and, after a moment's hesitation, grabbed the charging cable too. That computer, the keeper of all my half-finished essays, clearly came before my safety and wellness. Although if my computer burned, I would have a relatively valid reason for not completing the homework.

Not that any professor would accept that excuse. Still, a student could try.

Stumbling out of my dorm, I eventually made my way to the courtyard where everyone else was evacuating too. Other people were already congregating there, and I could see more spilling out. It always amazed me how the college could cram so many students into a single building. Like a clown car, though less funny. Unless there was free food, or if the fire alarm went off, we rarely all gathered. As far as I could see, there wasn't a charcuterie board in sight, but we unfortunately fulfilled the second condition.

Over the general chatter, I could hear one person muttering detailed threats of unique bodily harm about whoever set off the fire alarm. Must have been a Creative Writing major. Turning around, I spotted an older girl in a onesie with streaked make-up. Blue lipstick smeared her chin, while what was probably once a magnificent smoky eye now made her look like a panda.

An enraged panda.

So, running on a few hours of sleep and caffeinated fumes, I cheerfully approached and asked her what she meant. After all, the fire alarm only went off in extreme emergencies.

Right?

She rolled her eyes at my question. Reaching into her pocket, she pulled out some gummy bears and explained that the fire alarm rarely indicated an actual fire.

"Really?" I asked. At that point, I was a naïve first-year student. Even though I had already been through a couple of fire alarms, I had assumed each one was a life-or-death situation.

"Yeah," she responded, biting the head off a blue gummy bear. "The only actual emergency was when a stove caught fire in a different dorm."

Puzzled, I said that a stove was supposed to catch fire to work.

"Not so much that it burns the walls," she smirked. Elaborating, she explained that most of the time, the overly sensitive fire alarms were just set off by smoke in the dorms.

"Oh, like from candles?" I questioned.

Pausing mid-bite, she side-eyed me. "Yeah," she responded slowly. "From candles."

Throughout this exchange, the alarms continued to beep incessantly. Now and again, someone would loudly share their opinion on what had happened. Impassioned stories from their soapbox declarations slowly but surely trickled through the crowd.

Some said the fire could be on the third floor. Others swore it came from faulty wiring in the laundry room. One outlandish but popular theory was that someone had crawled onto the roof and lit something up there.

A few gossiped that the fire smelled like rotten eggs. Another group remarked it was more like the saccharine sweet odor of a Victoria's Secret perfume. Still, one student said it reeked of burnt cheese.

Rumors surrounding the apparently disastrous fire's victims also rippled through the increasingly cramped courtyard as more students dragged themselves out of the dorm. I overheard that everything from a student's fingertips to a new Spanish textbook–I winced in financial sympathy–had fallen prey to the flames.

Suddenly, the fire alarms stopped, and everyone went silent. Looking up, I saw a couple of campus police exit the building and turn to address the gathered students.

"Good morning, everyone," an officer started. "After investigating the dorms, we can confirm that the fire was caused by—"

With teary eyes, I turned to the onesie girl. "I hope everyone is okay," I exclaimed, rattled by the disastrous rumors.

"—an over-microwaved cup of mac and cheese. You may now return to your rooms."

The hush of shuffling slippers filled the courtyard in a slow shush. Sighing, the girl shoved her gummy bears back deep into her pocket and then glanced over at me.

"Still hope everyone's okay?" she asked smugly.

I was silent. If nothing else, I wanted her to have plausible deniability for whatever I would do to the monster who had been craving mac and cheese at the break of dawn.

-Teagan Durkin

Mom's New Meal Plan

OM'S FOLLOW-UP APPOINTMENT HAD gone pretty well. The doctor told me that her dementia was stable and to keep up with whatever I was doing. Dr. P's only suggestion was to increase Mom's calorie intake because she had lost a few pounds. Although it sounded simple enough, I knew it wouldn't be that easy. The nutritional drinks I had been passing off as strawberry milkshakes had stopped fooling her. She had probably spotted the empties in the recycling bin. It was also possible that she was using a hunger strike to get back at me for giving her a hard time as a kid. Either way, I needed to get this woman fattened up a bit!

We went home, and I racked my brain on how to proceed. I knew fast food wasn't the healthiest option, but it would certainly fit the calorie bill. Mom used to love the chicken sandwiches with all the condiments from our local place. I figured it was worth a try. That night at dinner, to my surprise, she ate the entire thing. I couldn't believe my eyes when I saw the empty plate sitting in front of her. I told her how proud I was of her for eating her whole meal and she seemed pleased with herself as well.

Later that evening, while watching TV, I looked over to see Mom yawning. It was time to tuck her in for the night. I escorted her to the bathroom, and as she sat down, I noticed a greasy napkin in her underwear. I grabbed the napkin and half of the chicken sandwich rolled onto the bathroom floor. Had she stashed it in her pants because she didn't like it? I'd like to think it was so good that maybe she was just trying to save some for later!

-Kelly Buchanan

The Blessing of Survivalist Skills

I N MAY 2001, WE purchased a heritage stone house in a bucolic village in mid-Western Ontario, Canada. The purchase had been under Power of Sale. As is.

This amazing home built in 1874 by Swiss immigrants needed a lifetime of work, something of which we were very cognizant, and, in fact, excited about. It was a project that would take us through middle age into our senior years.

It was a few days before closing. Our real estate agent was kind enough to let us have the keys, knowing we had a lot to overcome before we could move in. Cleaning was a considerable concern as the house had stood empty for eight years. My husband, who despite being a glass contractor, and quite handy with most reno-vations, has a remarkable distaste for spiders. Apparently, ridding the house of such nightmare-inducing vermin was the paramount task. Having been raised on a farm, he opted for agricultural-grade insecticide, which he liberally sprayed over every wall and floor on all three levels. Why use a little when you can use a lot to ensure complete eradication?

Now, in order for this tale to progress, it's important to under-stand the earlier phrase 'as is'. We did not know if the plumbing was okay, or the hot water heater, the furnace, the electrical system, in fact, anything that makes a house habitable. Does any of this bring to mind the 1986 comedy The Money Pit?

Knowing we needed to find out just how interesting our move-in date was going to be, we brought in a structural engi-neer, had the electrical and oil furnace assessed, and arranged for a plumber to meet us at the house the next day. We came armed with jerry cans of water, disinfectant cleaner, rags, mops, and such, hauled in a covered trailer, which carried all our re-enactment equipment.

Upon arrival, I set to washing all the walls and floors, starting on the second floor. There I discovered the agricultural-grade insecticide had left a thick, gray, greasy film over every surface. Have you ever tried to clean greasy surfaces with cold water? Yeah — really doesn't work. Just kind of smears everything around.

I suppose at this point I should point out there wasn't a level floor to be found anywhere in the house. I should also point out I wore thin tennis shoes, with no traction. Traction was exactly what I needed. As I was trying to mop a slippery floor, I slid inexorably toward the stairs, nothing to arrest my bumpy ride down to the first floor. Except my urgent cries for help.

Upon arriving safely on the first floor, it became apparent the only reasonable solution to the dilemma of greasy floors and walls was to create hot water. We were reenactors and backwoods campers of old. We knew about fire. We had cast iron enough to bring down castle walls. So, employing those traditional skills, we created ... FIRE!

Bringing into service our tripod and largest pot, I set about making a prodigious amount of hot water.

At that point, our plumber arrived to replace the one remaining piece of galvanized pipe in the basement. Should have been an easy one-hour job. Silly thought. Instead, that turned into all afternoon, discovery of a friction fit connection in the main bathroom tub (why use solder?), a smashed water meter, and an illegal and potentially hazardous hot water heater connection. There was also a geyser in the second sink tap (why were there two sinks in separate areas of the kitchen?), and two cracked toilets. As I was about to check on the fire, two strangers emerged from the basement door.

"Oh, hello? Who are you?"

"Is Bill here?"

"The plumber?"

"Yeah. We're from the Township."

"Ah, the water meter." I pointed in Bill's general direction, warned them about the floors, and escaped outside to a folding chair to watch a pot of water boil.

It was then the contractor we'd hired to build a shop for my husband's cooperage rounded the corner of the house. He came to an abrupt halt, seeing me sitting somewhat bedraggled and dazed by the fire, pot hung from the tripod, and said, "Rough day?"

The only sane response to that was to laugh. And laugh my husband and I did through moving day and the next two weeks. Not hysterical laughter. Not laughter of despair or frustration. It was the laughter of pure joy and adventure. We had this. We could do this. And for the past 22 years, that's just what we've done: lovingly, carefully, restore and renovate this remarkable heritage stone house. Knowing we're but the stewards of its history. And there's been quite a bit of laughter along the way.

-Lorina Stephens

Need For Speed

I WAS CERTAIN WE were going to be late for school...again.

It was a Thursday morning. I remember wearing a red top with a black vest, skirt, and wedges. Perhaps a bit much for a high school teacher, but I was dressed to win, equipped to dig in and get down to the joyful, and often thankless task of molding young minds. Well, except that I had to wait for my husband, The Man, to pick up the pace and get ready for work.

He had woken the kids up early to help get them ready for school. As usual, they'd gotten up before I eventually dragged myself from my bed into the kitchen to fix everyone's breakfast and pack the lunch. But I'd soon beat the clock, gotten dressed, fed the kids, and was ready to move; but my husband was taking his sweet time getting set.

So, I did what any reasonable wife would do. I left him to find his way to work while I took off with our only car, and set out on the six-minute journey, with our three kids, to their school, which so happened to be my workplace as well.

"Make sure you refuel the car," The Man said as I dashed out the door, without the usual goodbye kiss. "Don't forget to refuel."

He had a habit of repeating instructions, sometimes as much as three times, to drive a point home. I wanted to ignore him so that we could beat the first bell. However, when I glanced at the fuel gauge, while we bumped along the dirt road, I knew, even though we had less than five minutes left, I had to do as he'd instructed.

At the intersection, I noticed that our old beat-up car began spluttering, threatening, and demanding fuel. Behind me was one of the school buses taking our students to school. In front of me was a car that slowed a bit to cross into my side of the road—and zooming down the road from my left was a motorbike.

My life didn't flash before my eyes, but I did feel the jolt as the bike ran into my car. Leaving a considerable dent and also leaving me more than a bit shaken. Thankfully, all of us, including the bike rider and the friend with him, were fine.

It had taken all of twenty seconds from my remaining three minutes, so I quickly left the scene and drove into the petrol station. I parked the car, got out, still pretty frazzled, and then by some bigger stroke of ill luck, I couldn't get my fuel tank door open.

By then, I had negative five minutes left. A young man finally came to my help. We unlocked it, fueled the car, and I was ready to zoom off again. I turned the key in the ignition, but all I got was "click". The car just wouldn't budge.

I got more young men to help push the car to the side. With a flushed face and frail nerves, I called The Man and waited for him to come rescue us. I wasn't checking the time any longer. For all I cared, I could be forty, fifty minutes late. I didn't care anymore.

-Chiazo Obiudu

We Didn't Always Know How to Cook

RIGHT AFTER OUR WEDDING, Joy and I moved to Tennessee, where she studied missionary aviation, and I completed my student teaching. We did not have a lot of money. Everything Joy made from her nursing job went straight to pay for flight time. My third shift job packing boxes for a mail-order company paid for everything else. This left my $7.25 an hour job as our only income for gas, utilities, and groceries.

We ate cheap, meaning lots of rice and no beef. Our meats were chicken and what the grocery stores labeled as pork. Not pork chops, pork shoulder, or even pork butt. We bought pork. Everything went into a crock-pot because we both were out of the house during the day; but also because after six to eight hours in a crock-pot, any cut of meat is fall-apart tender. We also made iced tea. Gallon after gallon of iced tea. If there is an area between "I'll eat it I guess" and "Who put baking soda in the stew," my first few years of cooking fell right there.

By far, the worst meal I ever made was the yellow one. Every element of the dish turned out yellow, and then it got worse. Pan-fried Pork Chops with curried apple sauce, turmeric-seasoned rice, and roasted squash sounded good. Flight lessons in the afternoon meant Joy would be arriving home around six in the evening. I prepped, chopped, peeled, boiled, fried, and roasted. Never, ever had a meal been so perfectly timed out.

Our phone rang at 5:45. A last-minute student had called and wanted a lesson at six. Joy would be home at 7:30.

Cooking I could do, that was easy. But holding a meal that was already done until 7:30? This proved to be impossible. I tried; I really did.

The plate I handed Joy was yellow. Well, the plate itself was white, from the Garden Harvest Collection. But the food? All yellow, and by now after having been cooked, cooled, reheated, cooled again, and re-reheated all the same consistent mush. She tried to eat it but in the end, we both refused and ate ice cream.

Every family in the aviation program qualified for government food. Initially excited, we hoped this would augment our food budget, and, at times, it did. Big blocks of government cheese were always welcome. As were the loaves of bread from a local bakery. But the tall metal cans marked "MEAT?" No, they ended up a step too far. We took a few cans home the first time they appeared and stored them in our pantry. Neither of us knew what the cans held.

One day, we decided to try to make a stew with the canned meat. We chopped carrots, onions, and minced garlic. We opened the can of meat and both of us recoiled in horror. Inside the can, we saw white. Not pure snow-white but a dirty "snow has been on the ground a week and cars have driven through it" white. When I picked up the can, the fat rippled. Putting the can down, we both backed away from the table.

"I don't think that's the meat," I said, turning to my wife, who was on the verge of warding off evil as a defense.

"Poke it," she ordered.

"I'm not poking it, you poke it."

"Don't be a baby. Poke it." She gave me a long-handled fork.

Gingerly, I slid the fork into the can until it encountered something under the surface. As the fork was coming back out, the white mass on top broke into chunks and a brown liquid oozed forth. Fat. The white mass was the fat from the meat that had congealed on the surface. Joy made vomiting sounds. With a sucking sound, the fork finally cleared the fat, and on its tines was a piece of meat. Beef, pork, horse—to this day we have no idea what it was. It was squarish, reddish and I guess...meatish. In my wisdom, I thought if I shook it a little, some of the fat would fall out. The meat fell off the fork and plopped back into the can. Fat, gravy, and other stuff shot into the air and onto the kitchen table.

"I'm not eating that," I proclaimed.

"Maybe if we wash it off...." Joy's voice trailed off. "Dump that outside. We'll make vegetable and rice soup tonight."

-Bill Carrera

House Showing Fiasco

O NE NIGHT AFTER OUR two young children went to bed, my husband and I were enjoying some quality time together... on our phones. Like many nights before, my husband started showing me the dream houses on Zillow that he thought we should move to. Only, this time when he showed me a house, instead of laughing at him, I surprised him by saying, "Let's do it!"

We can be impulsive and don't like to waste time. So, less than 24 hours later, we saw the house, found an agent, and put an offer on it.

Red flags popped up during contract negotiations, so we backed out.

But, the idea of a new house stuck. We pressed forward, again wasting no time. Within the next week and a half, we visited 12 more houses, put an offer on a house, the new offer was accepted, signed a contract, and now only had 4 weeks to sell our current home and move.

No problem... right?

While my husband worked full time, I began the arduous challenge of selling our house and packing, while taking care of two young boys.

Thankfully, we had several interested buyers request showings. All I had to do was get the house clean.

To clear some of the mess, I started haphazardly throwing belongings into boxes. Which, of course, seemed to always fly straight back out at the hands of a curious child. I would clean one mess, to turn around and see two more.

As time crept by, I was getting more and more stressed. What on earth had we gotten ourselves into?

Again, I would clean and clean. Find more messes. Repeat.

We were down to one last hour before it was time for the showings. I was so close.

I was walking down the stairs when I looked toward my kitchen. Separating our front room and our kitchen, there was a pony wall. One of those pointless short walls that doesn't reach the ceiling. And it was so dusty and dirty on top. There was no way I could leave it for the showings.

My youngest son needed to be fed before I could get it done. I was confident that I could get both tasks accomplished in time for the showings.

My son does not eat by mouth. Because of physical and mental challenges, he eats fully by G-Tube. (A tube that enters directly through his stomach, bypassing his mouth.) We place the formula in a machine, which then pumps it directly into his stomach. Feedings this way are time-consuming, so we put his machine in a little backpack that he wears while he plays around. Cute and efficient.

I got my son's feeding set up, climbed a ladder, and cleaned.

Minutes later, my older son told me the floor was wet. I ignored him.

A few more minutes passed and my son told me the couch was wet now too.

Finally registering what he said, I looked down to see that my younger son had removed the feeding tube from his stomach and it was leaking all over the front room.

A giant vanilla-scented mess.

I quickly turned to climb down the ladder to stop the flow of food, when...

The ladder disappeared!

My older son, desperate to help me during this crazy moment accidentally knocked over the ladder.

Here I stood on top of a tall, yet somehow not tall enough, wall. I had one child running around the room leaking formula all over the floor and furniture. Another child standing in the corner crying because all he wanted to do was help. The clock quickly ticking down the moments until potential buyers would walk into this mess. What was I supposed to do?

Really, there was only one thing I could do. Jump.

I did my best to gather my nerves and moved closer to the couch. Hopefully, that would soften my fall.

Then I jumped!

Ouch.

Seems I miscalculated life — again. I landed on the hard floor covered with toys. Not even close to the couch I aimed for.

There was no time for pain. Moving faster than should be possible at that moment, I got moving. I stopped my son's food from splattering every surface in the house, used my beloved carpet cleaner to clean the spills, and prayed the visitors would think the lingering vanilla scent was a candle. All the while, both my sons screamed and cried in the background.

With only minutes to spare, I grabbed what I needed to head to the car with my boys. While running down the stairs to head out the front door, I slammed to a stop.

That pony wall.

I never finished it.

In fact, I made it way worse.

Now, the top of the wall was half cleaned, leaving the other dirty half glaringly, obtrusively obvious.

Time was out. I had to leave it.

We went to the car to drive around the neighborhood during the showings.

Not wanting to go too far, because, of course, I had to stalk our potential buyers.

Only, as we waited; no one came.

Thirty minutes, an hour, two hours.

The first showing group never showed up...

(Kids crying in the car)

The second showing group never showed up...

(Kids crying in the car)

The third showing group never showed up...

(Kids crying in the car, begging to go home.)

When finally, the fourth showing group showed up.

I was so happy I was going to cry! (We are pretending like I wasn't already stress-crying right along with my boys)

But the group never went into the house.

My phone vibrated, and I looked down to see a text from our agent.

"The fourth showing group has decided the neighborhood does not fit what they are looking for and they are going to pass. "

The group pulled away from my house, taking with them the last bit of my sanity.

Sore and tired, I walked back into my house and just sat there.

Even my boys deflated, seeming to understand it was all for nothing.

With perfect timing, my husband walked in the door from work, eager to hear how everything went.

He took one look at our exhausted faces, one sniff of the vanilla aroma, and said,

"Oh no. What happened?"

A few weeks later, as we sat amid piles of boxes in our new house, all we could do was laugh. It was 6 weeks to the day from when my husband routinely showed me a pretty house, with no intention of it going anywhere. Though the days were easy to count, the number of fiascos and tears spent during that time was too high to put a number on. But we survived it. And now we were home. With lots of new crazy days to laugh about for years to come.

-Amilee Weaver Selfridge

Major Life Events With a Side of Sushi

IT WAS THE NIGHT of my 17th birthday. As usual, we had the siblings over (including my brother's fiancé), my sister made an epic cake, and I chose the wonderful dish sushi for my birthday dinner.

As my sister and I went on our adventure to obtain the sacred sushi, I began feeling quite nauseous. This wasn't too out of the blue, seeing as how I get car sick anytime I'm in a car while not driving. But this was a little stronger than usual. I brushed it off, as most people do, celebrated my birthday, and didn't feel nauseous for the rest of the night. At least, the rest of the night until 3 o'clock in the morning, when I rushed down to the bathroom and made that my humble abode until the sun rose and my mother awoke. Now this seemed like just a regular old case of the stomach bug, not very fun to have on your birthday, but also not all that interesting to write about. However, dear reader, what makes this specific incident so memorable is that it just so happened, the day after my birthday, was the day of my brother's wedding!

The first child in my family to find someone to spend the rest of their life with got married, and I completely missed it. While my entire family celebrated the union of two people while eating dry cake, I was slowly dying on the living room couch in my horse-printed pajamas. This is a sorrowful tale, I know, but when it really comes down to it, the truly tragic part of this dilemma is—I can no longer eat the excellent dish sushi without getting nauseous.

-J. A. Norman

To Be, or Not to Be

I T WAS THE BEGINNING of a long, sweltering summer in Texas when I applied for a stockman's position at the local convenience store near the house. The pay was not all that great, but I knew it would provide for me to buy some new clothes for college.

Since an early age, I have always been independent and wanted to earn my way. It gave me a sense of pride and accomplishment, knowing that I worked hard and got paid at the end of the day. Some days, I would borrow my mother's car, but many days I would trek about a mile to work. It was not too bad; I was young and energetic. and besides, it kept me in great shape. I would get up during the week around 8:00 a.m. and be a work until 10:00 p.m. After my first check, I went to buy some new clothes. I purchased some new jeans and polo shirts, then shoes, and finally several new sports jackets and slacks, then one suit. It did not take long before summer was almost over and I would head back to Atlanta, GA for college. I looked forward to wearing all the new gear for classes.

When I arrived at the airport, I caught a cab to the campus.

"Your dorm room is not ready to be moved in yet," said the admission clerk. "Come back this afternoon."

"What will I do with all of my luggage,"

I called a friend of my father to pick me up. He stated that he would keep my luggage in his car until I finished all my business for school. About two hours later, my dorm room was ready, so I called my father's friend to return to campus. As his car pulled in, I could not see any of my luggage.

"Where is my luggage?" I asked with a strange expression on my face. "I know there were three bags of clothes."

"You sure did," replied my father's friend.

"What happened?"

After a long day of looking for my luggage, I came to the realization that all was lost and that somebody had stolen all that I valued.

I never found my luggage and all of my brand-new clothes were gone forever

"What will I do?" I asked myself.

My new roommates could tell something was very wrong. I did not want to talk, play, or even be at school.

I called my father about the incident. "Son, don't worry, I have lost fortunes in my life... I will wire you some money to get some new clothes."

That made me feel a little better, and that all was not lost. Days later, I got the money and went right out to purchase some new clothes. There was a sale at the mall, so I got a lot of really nice things cheap.

About a week later, I got a call from my big brother, Keith. "I am sending you some things since we are the same size," said Keith. "I am sending you my nice blue pin stripped suit, the one I love. However, when you get back home, I want it back."

I soon realized that college life was a series of challenges, ups and downs. It is not what happens to you, but it is all how you respond. So, as my mentor and friend Shakespeare once said, "To Be or Not to Be, that is the question.

-*Geary Smith*

Wireless

R EYNARD WAS ALWAYS A tornado of energy, incapable of staying still in one place for too long. He was quick to explain, as he put it, his condition.

"I have ADHD, you see, so I can't help that I'm frenzied and frenetic most of the time," my thirteen-year-old brother explained to his latest girlfriend while we were waiting at Burger King. Laylah gazed adoringly at him while he spoke energetically to her.

"If I sit still for too long, it's like... I don't know, I feel smothered, you know? Or maybe like I'm drowning. Do you get it?" Reynard asked Laylah.

Is she even listening to my infuriating brother?

I rolled my eyes in exasperated annoyance. Reynard could be such a dork most of the time. Being his little sister had its advantages though, like this free meal I got because Laylah wasn't allowed to go out alone with Reynard.

"Uh-huh. I totally get it, Reynard. I promise you I do," pumpkin pips for brains, Laylah swiftly responded.

"Oh, okay. That's good. But you know what? The only thing that calms me down is music. That's why I love to listen to the music on my phone whenever the world becomes too slow for me," Reynard confessed. "Isn't that true, Tracy?" Dragging me into his yawn of a conversation with Laylah.

"Huh?" I said, immediately regretting that I sounded dumb. "Yeah, that's true. Only music can calm Reynard down," I admitted. Then I added, "But only the music of Michael Jackson. Reynard loves Michael Jackson to death!"

"Shut up, Tracy, and eat your burger before I feed it to the gulls!" Reynard rudely threatened me, pointing at the greedy gulls circling outside the restaurant.

Suddenly, Laylah perked up. "Did you hear about the new wireless earphones?" she eagerly asked Reynard, her voice rising excitedly. "Apparently, they are called Bluetooth earphones. They don't use wires at all. I don't exactly know how they work, but I heard you just plug the earphones into your ears and the music will play directly from your phone into your ears!"

"Wow!" Reynard exclaimed. "Technology's really awesome nowadays," he added. "I'm so glad I wasn't born in an earlier time."

"You can say that again!" Laylah agreed.

"Ok," Reynard said before he repeated himself. "I'm so glad I wasn't born in an earlier time."

I choked on a bite of burger as I laughed at how literal my brother could be.

Laylah wrinkled her button nose in confusion.

"She didn't mean it literally, you goofball! It's an expression, and it means she agrees with you," I said, unable to stop myself from correcting Reynard.

He gave me a dark glare, making me think maybe I had gone too far this time. Fortunately, infatuated Laylah came to my rescue.

"It doesn't matter if he's a goofball. He's still adorable," Laylah declared before leaning over the table to swiftly kiss Reynard on his lips. I groaned in mock disgust at this display.

"Shut it, you!" Reynard told me, his gaze still hot, promising me dire torment and torture later. I wisely shut it.

We walked Laylah home-Reynard was old-fashioned like that. Upon returning home, we found our parents relaxing in the lounge. Mom, head buried in some novel. Dad watching a televised soccer match.

I threw myself down next to Mom on the sofa. Dad in his recliner, of course.

"Dad, did you hear about the new Bluetooth earphones?" Reynard said, "Laylah told me about them today and she says they're the best!"

I knew Dad was only listening with a quarter of an ear; I grinned when he absent-mindedly replied, "Sure, Reynard. No worries. Go ask your brother."

"Cool! Thanks, Dad," Reynard said and went looking for Hugh, our older brother. I jumped up to follow Reynard because I knew what Hugh's answer would be. A resounding, "No!" I didn't want to miss the fun of seeing Reynard's disappointment.

Reynard stormed into Hugh's bedroom without even knocking, but lucky for him, Hugh wasn't in his room. Just as Reynard was about to leave the room, he spotted Hugh's pair of earphones hanging over the computer monitor.

"Don't you even dare!" I cautioned Reynard.

"Shut up, squirt!" he barked at me before grabbing the earphones. "These will work great!" Reynard said excitedly.

Then he went straight to the kitchen to get a pair of scissors, me in tow. With two swift snips, Reynard separated the earphones from the wire.

"Hugh's gonna kill you dead," I gasped. Reynard just ignored me.

Eagerly, like a child with a new toy, Reynard inserted the now "wireless" earphones into his ears as he played a song on his phone.

"Wow! This is awesome!" Reynard enthused before singing along at the top of his voice to MJ's "Beat It".

I followed him as he took off for his bedroom, but on his way, he passed through the lounge again. Hugh had by then joined Mom and Dad in the sitting room. All three looked up in astonishment at Reynard, happily belting out his favorite song, which was playing on his phone, of course.

"What the heck are you doing?" Hugh was the first to ask, his tone revealing his utter incredulity. He hadn't yet noticed that Reynard using his now-severed earphones. They were just all disturbed by Reynard's loud, off-key screeching.

"I'm listening to music via Bluetooth, bro! I'm surprised you didn't know you don't need to plug the cable in to use the earphones," Reynard informed Hugh, grinning like the Cheshire Cat.

I gleefully waited for the inevitable explosion.

Abruptly, all three noticed what Reynard had done to Hugh's earphones. Mom threw herself on the floor, cry-laughing with amusement. Dad slapped his forehead and mumbled, "This dumb kid." Hugh's face turned crimson before he jumped up in fury.

"You destroyed my Apple, original earphones, Genius! You're gonna buy me new ones, or else!" he threatened, before throwing up his hands in defeat and stomping off to his bedroom.

"Ah, my oh-so-clever clown of a brother," I said as I joined Mom on the floor, offering her a Kleenex to wipe away her tears.

"What did I do?" Reynard asked, completely mystified.

-Hidayat Adams

Relocation Blues

OH NO, A TEXT from my landlord. Is this the rent increase I've dreaded? Yes, in the depths of winter, almost three months before my lease was up, there it was, a completely "non-negotiable" $150.00 monthly hike. Between that and the leaky windows causing sky-high gas bills, I knew my time in my second-floor two-bedroom "penthouse" with views of the mountains was up. He also had recently said that any ordinary wear and tear was up to the tenant to fix. Yeah, sure. I went on Next Door and messaged someone wanting to sublet her $300.00 cheaper (before the rent hike) apartment, a smaller one-bedroom. It was a little over a mile away, further from my favorite coffee house than I wanted to be, but hey, the timing was right. The landlady told me the rent included the gas and electric expenses. To borrow from the Jeffersons, I was "moving on down, from the southeast side..."

On moving day, running a bit late on packing the last couple of boxes, I checked outside to see if the movers had come or were in transit, if they were running a little late themselves. Nothing. After that, I tried calling the head guy. No answer. I had put my cat in her carrier in the tub in the bathroom to have her out of the way of the movers. After a few hours of non-response, I thought, well, I have one more day before my lease is up—I had planned ahead—maybe I should find another mover. I signed up with another company, from the nearby big city. They would charge more and extra for the mileage to my place. In the late afternoon, I finally reached the original mover. "Where are you?"

"What do you mean? I have you scheduled for April 2."

"Really? "

That date was from a move years ago, in an old email. I had confirmed the current day in another email a week ago. He said "yes," in reply. I thought we were literally on the same page. I had today's date in the subject line and in the body of the email. He said he could come over tomorrow in the a.m.

After canceling the other movers, thankfully, with a refundable deposit, early the next morning, I attempted to stuff Le Chat back into her carrier. Luring her into the bathroom proved difficult, as she noticed her carrier sitting in the tub. No way, she half-growled, looking away. Okay, I grabbed her in the hallway and literally stuffed her into the top opening of the carrier. She wanted to fight me, but phew, I escaped major scratches and she only lost a little hair. Aside from a maximum of meowing, our struggle ended with her zipped up in her carrier. Right on time, the movers arrived.

"Would it be possible to put the boxes in their correct rooms?"

"No, because we wouldn't be able to move the furniture in then."

"How about if they moved the boxes after the furniture?" I thought to myself. Then (out loud) "How about, since the boxes are each labeled by room and contents, stack them in piles according to proper room?"

"Okay, sure."

I guess I'd see how that worked out. Despite multiple visits from the Salvation Army guys to pick up extra books, artwork, clothes, and furniture, I must have packed 100 boxes.

As the truck arrived in the new place's lot, the head mover, Mac, wanted a neighbor to move her car to give his truck more room. She didn't answer her door, so the landlady placed a call, finding out that she wasn't returning until the next day. I asked Mac if he would be okay and he said yeah, but "if something gets scratched, it's not my fault."

Oh, great. After refusing to put the boxes in the room they belonged, each one labeled, and color-coded, he began advising me on where to put each piece in the living room. "Oh, you want your TV over there?"

"No, it would block the view."

"What view? The wall?... Your couch needs to go there."

I disagreed. "No, I want it here. That's where the former tenant had it."

"But you're better than her."

"True." Uh-huh, I'm better than the young opera singer with curly auburn hair who is moving for a better job to Austin with her boyfriend. Just put it where I want it, Mac.

"Your table needs to go here and I'll tell you why," he said. "Your kitchen will be right next to it."

I guess I hired a "full-service" guy: therapist, interior designer, furniture mover—all in one,

When Mac and his two helpers left, I brought the cat in from the car, and after opening the carrier, reclined on the couch for a breather. Le Chat had to explore each room before joining me, curling up on my midsection as usual. From my position to my right, there was a wall of boxes, taking up half a long living room; cardboard containers, each row stacked four, five, and six high. Yikes, well, at least I had labeled not only the room, to no avail, but the contents. I think Mac may have grouped them according to room request, somewhat, anyway. I found most of the essentials to start living, some packed in my car, or in special boxes, the plastic ones, easy to identify.

Better start the new Salvation Army pile, that is, if and when I can get up from the couch.

-Andee Baker

I Do Dumb Things

WITH THE TEMPERATURE DROPPING, plants needed to come inside. I tried to work a little outside and then gave up. It was too nippy. I figured I'd tackle some indoor chores instead. First, I replaced my Halloween flag with a Charlie Brown Thanksgiving banner. Before stowing the Halloween flag away for next year, I'd carry it downstairs to wash. While upstairs, I meandered down to the bonus room atop the garage to pick up three large packages of 12-roll toilet paper. We'd kept them in storage since the early days of the pandemic. Our downstairs bathrooms were out. Then, I happened to spy an old dead orchid in my late dad's bathroom, adjacent to the bonus room. (Dad had been gone for ten years. I did water that plant from time to time.) So, I grabbed the shriveled plant to dispose of outside. With all the stuff gathered in my hands, I started down the back stairs. Guess what! Like my late mom and my grown daughter, I suffer from DROPSIES! For no reason at all, I dropped the dozens of rolls of toilet paper, the decorative flag, and yes, of course, the plant—causing dry dirt to spew all over the stairs, floor, walls, and the Persian carpet!

To rectify this mishap, I snatched my hand vacuum cleaner that I never used, but Marisol appeared to use it every two weeks when she came. Well, the dang thing disappointingly wouldn't suck up the smallest speck of soil. I ended up using my hands! After twenty minutes, I sort of, maybe, kind of cleaned it up, but the carpet didn't look good. Anyway, I went to empty the thing-a-ma-jig, and it refused to empty. I yelled for my husband, who was out cleaning the pool (a real job) before the first frost arrived. He sallied in and tinkered with the gadget; pried it open and yanked out this awful, mangey thing with strings wrapped around it. A dead mouse! No, a baby's sock! I figured that was from July Fourth or maybe last December when the grandkids visited! I guess Marisol thought the vacuum do-hickey would pick up anything, unless, of course, I was the culprit who scooped up the sock? Could be. I daydream when cleaning. The other vacuum like it broke during the holidays, and my oldest bought me this one at Walmart for Christmas. So, it wasn't that old. Hmm. Was the other one really broken, or did Marisol... or I vacuum up socks?

After the calamity with the dropsies and spending 40 more minutes to finish the simple tasks, I was tuckered out. What did I have to show for it? A ruined rug.

My conclusion, my take-away message, the theme of this little anecdote is obvious: I was not made to work! I'm such a disorganized goofball! And klutz! But I deduced another lesson from my doomed ability to clean up the smallest of messes. One should never get on too high a horse when ordinary projects can humble you in a heartbeat—or in the time it takes for a bundle of junk to leap out of your arms and tumble down a flight of stairs.

-Erika Hoffman

It Seemed Like a Good Idea

I WIPED THE SWEAT out of my eyes and got white paint on my forehead. My job today was painting rocks. The teenagers around me were fitting painted rocks into two big C's on the hill for Camp Christy. Why had it ever seemed like a good idea to come to a Gospel camp in the middle of nowhere Kansas? All the other camps my dad ran had dark wild forests and deep lakes. We couldn't even go swimming in the pool until the painting crew finished working on that. Why had I said I would go with my dad to a teen work camp instead of staying at a babysitter for a week? Here, everyone treated me like a kid. I was twelve, surrounded by huge teen boys and teenage girls who seemed so grown up.

It was at the water break that my father said, "I need volunteers for a special project." I put my hand up, along with almost everyone else. "No, honey. I need the tall guys for this." He measured the tallest five guys. "Ok, we also need a crew to tear down the old outhouse on top of the hill." This time, he nodded that I could come. "Then the rest can finish painting the rocks."

I joined Mike and Dan, the shortest of the football players, along with a couple of other girls.

"You only got to be here because he's your dad," Mike said as we got tools. "I don't know why we need five people; Dan and I can knock down that tiny thing over by ourselves. The rest of you just stay out of our way." Dan and Mike flexed their football muscles to warm up, and each grabbed a sledgehammer. I sighed, put the nail-puller I used as a crowbar on my shoulder, and hung the water cooler on it. We hiked to the top of the hill.

We gathered around the tiny one-seater. "What do we do after we knock it down?"

Mike asked.

My dad smiled and checked us for work gloves and safety goggles. "This was the first building here; built by the very first work camp." We looked over the cartoon-perfect outhouse with a crescent moon on the door and a little 'occupied' sign that flipped up when the door was closed. We all wondered what the campers had done before they finished the outhouse. None of us dared ask. "Now the paneling should go here. Most of the nails are junk, but if you find any long ones or square ones, save them. Be careful." He smiled and led his crew away.

It hit us. We needed to be careful and not just smash it.

I sat on the ground and started prying on the nails on the bottom door hinge. Mike tapping on the underside of the roof.

When I got the door off the hinges, I glanced at my watch. It had been an hour. Mike didn't even have all the shingles off. We only had a little pile of nails, boards, and a lot of broken bits of plywood. My hands were blistered, and I learned that nails driven into plywood can take ten minutes to pull out. "Water break," Dan called. We settled on the dry grass and gazed at the shade from the cottonwood trees at the bottom of the hill.

"It'd be a lot better to do this down there," one girl said.

"Why don't we?" I said excitedly.

"Why don't we, what?" Mike said.

"Take it apart down there," I said. "You hear about people tipping over outhouses all the time."

"No way. It's on a cement foundation." Dan said. One of the many mysteries we had been afraid to ask about. Why did those first campers think an outhouse needed a cement floor and thick plywood walls? We understood the toilet seat and lid.

Mike grinned. "All we have to do is saw off the corner posts. Give me the saws." Only minutes later, Dan and Mike backed up, bent down, and charged. The posts splintered, and cracked, and the whole outhouse tipped and slowly slid downhill. We cheered. "There's a stump," one girl yelled. My stomach twisted. The outhouse hit the stump; flipped end-over-end and cartwheeled down the hill. We followed, whooping and hollering. We had found a great way to get those stubborn shingles off. It went past the patch of shade and kept going down the hill.

"The garage," Mike yelled. We froze and stared. The outhouse slammed into the garage upside down and shuddered into a pile of boards. We ran down the hill, gathering up what the outhouse dropped.

As the painting crew came in, we were neatly stacking boards. We had a pile of broken boards and I volunteered to help Mike carry some to the camp burn barrel. I love a good fire. We dropped them in and then we smelled something, something horrible. Like a rotted skunk, outhouse, and something else.

"Out of the way," a voice yelled. We jumped to the side and kept moving as one of the tall guys walked toward the burn barrel with some cloth dangling on the end of a long pole. My dad followed him with a can of gas. He waved us away after the cloth dropped in and the guy joined us. My dad poured the gas and lit it. The smell doubled for a moment, and we all ran back.

We all stared at my dad; just then, three of the tall guys came around the corner from the shower building. "We got him in the shower, but it didn't help." The smell coming out of the shower building.

By this time, all the kids and adults were hanging around, carefully downwind from the black smoke oozing out of the burn barrel.

My Dad spoke first, "We were looking for that old septic tank. I knew it was only five feet deep. It was all covered in plants and sand. And well," he sighed and glanced to the shower building. "Johnny found it."

"Yeah, by the boards breaking and him falling in." One boy said.

Beside me, Mike gulped, "First time I'm glad I'm short." I nodded.

"OK, girls. Go find some good, scented shampoo," my dad said. "And then get to the snack bar. I'm giving everyone a five-buck credit."

I joined the boys charging for the snack bar. I decided on a 50-cent soda and three candy bars and was calculating what else to get: when the three boys came in, shaking their heads. "It didn't work. Now he smells like flowers on..." They glanced at my father. "A septic tank."

I drank the rest of my soda and took my credit slip to my cabin. On the bottom of my shower bag was the bottle I kept hidden. I walked back to the snack bar with it and handed it to one of the boys. "Here, try this." I hoped none of the girls noticed the letters on the bottle, For Extreme Dandruff.

He took the bottle as my dad was rounding everybody up and leading us to the dining hall to play indoor games before supper.

About twenty minutes later, Johnny walked in. He didn't look bad, just wrinkly and he didn't smell bad. "There's no hot water left." There were groans. He handed me back my half-empty bottle. "Thanks. At least I won't have to worry about dandruff." I braced for the laughter, but all the boys in his cabin cheered.

-Joyce Frohn

FOR BETTER OR WORSE- WAS THAT A THREAT...

Are there any available upgrade options?

Honeymoon (Turquoise) Blues

A T THREE IN THE morning, my brand-new husband, Jon, and I would soon leave for our honeymoon in Barbados. But something was wrong.

"Does your stomach feel like it's about to explode too?" I whispered, wondering if he was awake.

He answered with a groan and ran downstairs to the one bathroom in the house. I hoped I wouldn't have to fight him for it.

I thought back to everything we'd eaten since the wedding. If we were both sick, it had to be something we both ate. I ruled out the dairy items since Jon is lactose intolerant and I'm not. Maybe it was the hors d'oeuvres served at the beginning of the reception. They sat out the longest and the caterer packed the leftovers for us to take home. It was possible they'd turned.

At 4:30 a.m., my (new) mother-in-law picked Jon and me up to take us to the airport. With her was my sister-in-law, brother-in-law, and toddler niece, who'd come to town for the wedding and had an early flight out. Jon insisted on driving because, as sweet as she is, his mother's driving makes me motion sick under the best circumstances. He drove slowly and carefully out of consideration for our stomachs.

The opossum didn't get the message.

As Jon took the exit toward the airport, a massive opossum crossed the ramp at that exact moment. Jon jerked the wheel, narrowly avoiding hitting its hissing face and dozens of pointy, sharp teeth. Though I was glad we didn't hit the opossum, my stomach might not have lurched so violently if we had.

"Pull over!" I shouted.

"Right now?" Jon asked, incredulous.

"RIGHT NOW!"

I was out of the van before we'd come to a complete stop. Mere hours after officially becoming part of my husband's family, they watched me wretch over the side of a guardrail.

"You okay? You need anything?" Jon asked, suddenly beside me.

"Water," I coughed.

He rooted around in the van for what seemed like a long time while I stood there trying to decide if I might wretch again.

Jon returned with my toddler niece's sippy cup.

"It's the only drink we have," he said.

"I can't take a bottle from a baby!" I said, flabbergasted. What would my in-laws think?!

"This is all we have," Jon said, shrugging.

I assessed the taste in my mouth and prayed my niece wouldn't remember the day her aunt took her sippy cup.

"Wait!" I said, the bottle at my lips. "This isn't breastmilk, right?"

"Of course not!" my sister-in-law hollered from inside the vehicle.

Back in the van, it was eerily quiet, which only added to my embarrassment. So, I broke the ice.

"Well," I said drily. "I didn't expect that 'in sickness and in health' clause to kick in so soon!"

Everyone laughed, and the awkwardness dissipated. We talked about how surely this would be the strangest story to come out of our honeymoon.

But my in-laws didn't see what happened after we parted ways at the airport.

At the check-in counter, I learned that my husband—whom I'd been engaged to for two years and dated for two years before that—had mistyped my middle name. Which is three letters long.

"You mean you don't know how to spell my middle name?!"

Jon swore it was a typo and that he really did know how to spell it, but the agent would not let me on the plane.

"Sir, you have to let me on the plane! It's our honeymoon and we're going to Barbados. And it was expensive to book and we're only planning on getting married just this once and I've already barfed on the side of the road this morning and..." I begged. I pleaded. I cried.

The agent looked warily at Jon, probably wondering how well we knew each other before getting married if he fudged my middle name on my plane tickets. But after twenty minutes, we convinced the powers to be that be that it really was just an honest mistake––and they let us board.

Once on the plane, we breathed a sigh of relief. We were on the plane, headed to our honeymoon destination. Plane crashes are fairly rare, so we thought nothing else could go wrong. Our week together in tropical wedded bliss could finally begin! We watched the sunrise over the Caribbean and marveled at the turquoise water, knowing we'd be swimming in it soon enough.

When the plane landed in Barbados, the salty island air brushed our faces and arms––so much more refreshing than the air in Ohio. I couldn't wait to get our bags and head straight to the resort's beachfront.

Except that our bags weren't there.

We waited and waited and waited at the carousel. My distinctive black rolling suitcase with red roses polka dotting its surface never materialized. Of all the times for an airline to lose luggage...

"My swimsuit was in there," I whimpered, officially at my wits' end.

Ever practical, Jon went into *I'll handle this* mode and filed a report for our missing luggage while I let myself have a good frustration cry.

A shuttle took us to the resort, where we were greeted with songs and flutes of champagne we were still too sick to drink, but sipped anyway.

Jon and I went to bed early to recover from the tiring day. Two days, later a knock at our room door revealed a bellhop with our suitcase––minus one of its roller wheels so that it had to be dragged instead of rolled.

When the bellhop left, Jon and I collapsed into laughter. This wasn't how we thought our honeymoon would go, but there was no one I'd rather share a week in paradise with. Without Jon, it wouldn't be paradise at all. In sickness and in health, in potential roadkill and saved critters, in misspelled middle name and new last name, in roller luggage with three wheels, till death do us part.

And now that we had our suitcase with our swimwear, we could finally soak in that bright turquoise water.

-Mandy Shunnarah

Rehearsal Dinner Calamity

M Y FOCUS AS A bride had been intent on wedding day plans, so I was completely caught off guard when the rehearsal dinner the night before the ceremony spun completely out of control.

I hired the banquet hall of a reputable, local hotel. I had the foresight to prepay for sixteen catered meals, so I expected a leisurely, uneventful gathering with my attendants before they retired early to prepare for the next day's festivities.

The first sign of trouble was when I walked into an unnaturally busy hotel lobby. To my chagrin, unchaperoned teenagers zoomed around the hotel hallways on bicycles. While ushering me to the dining area, the staff informed me that a Bicycle Motor Cross convention was in progress.

My anxious Maid of Honor then informed me that some of my party was not coming to the dinner. Apparently, during the rehearsal at the church, a groomsman's wife became jealous of her husband's happy interaction with one of my bridesmaids. The dinner was evidently being boycotted by some of my new in-laws. I asked the head waiter if he could delay the meal in the hopes my guests would decide to join us, but he informed me my party had the banquet room for an allotted time.

Just as we sat down to put knives in our steaks, the hotel fire alarm blared.

Frantic employees herded wedding guests, bicyclists, and complaining hotel patrons to the safety of the outside pool area.

My party patiently waited on the patio on that scorching summer evening as the staff went room to room to determine if there truly was a fire. Speculation quickly grew that a prankster, a teenage bicyclist pulled one of the fire alarms.

Worried eyes lifted toward the skies as dark clouds grumbled overhead. Anxious glances were exchanged between my elegantly coffered bridesmaids who had spent the afternoon at the hair salon.

A groomsman volunteered to rush to the parking lot to retrieve umbrellas from his car, but before his return, sheets of rain poured from the heavens. My friends made certain the bride had the most shelter as we backed up under the scant protection of the roof eaves.

And then more unexpected mayhem. Some well-meaning local officials had ordered the police helicopter to investigate a possible fire at a crowded hotel. Cries of panic ensued as the chopper hovered over the pool. It blasted the wedding party with a spray of water as the spinning blades stirred up a whirlwind.

They waved the helicopter off. The rain stopped.

My bedraggled groom and I stood staring at one another in profound disbelief.

I suppose he and my guests would have completely understood if the bride went berserk at that moment, but I remained calm. I had waited a long time to marry my man and nothing, absolutely nothing, was going to ruin this celebration for us.

No sign of a fire inside the hotel, so our wedding party returned to the banquet hall.

Following my lead, my guests calmly took their seats at the table. We dried off with dinner napkins—extra napkins available because of the settings still in place for our no-show guests. We proceeded to eat our cold meal in stunned silence.

The nervous head waiter leaned over and whispered into my ear. I think he had braced for an explosion when he informed this pushed-too-far bride that my party's time at the banquet hall was about the expire. We had fifteen minutes to finish our meal before the next customer arrived.

I just nodded and chewed.

After I said good night to our wonderful, uncomplaining guests, my fiancé escorted me to my vehicle. He opened his mouth once to speak. There seemed no words to say. He kissed my cheek, and we parted for the night.

To this day I can conjure the sight when my overly dramatic Maid of Honor burst into the church dressing room the next morning and excitedly announced, "He came! He actually came!"

My bridesmaids had speculated that the horrific portents of doom that occurred during our disastrous rehearsal dinner would have made any sane man reconsider going through with the wedding.

But my groom smiled when he greeted me at the altar. Later I understood it was my grace in the face of calamity that reassured him that we could make this marriage work no matter the disasters we faced in the future.

The wedding ceremony was flawless, complete with the attendants who had boycotted our rehearsal dinner. A joyous reception luncheon immediately followed the ceremony and proceeded without a major mishap. The honeymoon trip was fantastic.

And my husband and I have been happily married for thirty-eight years.

-Cheryl Anderson Davis

The Hex of the Ex

THE PHONE RANG INCESSANTLY, and I knew who was calling. I had cried for an hour after receiving the first call. Still working on toughening up, I answered in a mildly quivering voice, "Hello?"

After moments of silence, he answered, "I got drunk, I can't bear it myself!" Had it been an incident from my recent forty-something years and not from two decades ago, I would have laughed out loud. He was overdoing the slur, rolling his R's effectively, but quite unconvincingly.

And what could he not bear? That he visited my city for a wedding and called me to make several excuses about why he couldn't meet for lunch, dinner, or coffee? Or that once he was back, safely ensconced in his own apartment, in a different part of the country, he called me to explain why he was breaking up with me after five years. Apparently, his dad had a heart attack because he wouldn't say 'yes' to the marriage proposal his dad wanted him to pursue.

Classic Bollywood! Done, re-done, and overdone. The thing was, I had grown up watching the same movies. I knew how the plot unfurled.

"Did you eat?" he asked, trying to sound tearful and broken-hearted beyond repair. "Are you okay?"

"Why wouldn't I be? I finished dinner an hour ago.." I answered, keeping the anger out of my voice. I would not give him the satisfaction of knowing how distraught I felt.

"Oh! That's... that's good! I'm glad...you... you're okay," he stuttered, forgetting the pronounced slur that he was faking minutes ago. There was a moment of awkward silence. Actually, the silence was that of mourning. My trust in him had died.

I glanced at the dusty clock ticking away lazily overhead. It was almost 11 p.m., and I wanted to end this pointless conversation with the man who recently gained X-boyfriend status. Catching a little ticklish yawn forming somewhere in the space between my nostrils, I used it. Making it as loud as possible, I said in my best, fake-groggy voice, "I hope I can finish the movie I was watching before I sleep..."

"You were watching a movie?" he asked, rather surprised. *Yay! Another hit.* He had first called to break the news at around 6:30 in the evening. Until the second call around 10:45 pm, I had been crying silly, in bouts, gasping, cursing him, myself, the universe, and wallowing in self-pity. I had no interest in watching a movie. The last thing I wanted was to have people talking and moving around me, even televised ones! I wanted to feel solitary, distant, detached from everything and everyone I knew.

However, I did eat dinner, that part was not made up. Food is sustenance and one needs sustenance, even more so during a break-up. A humiliating one over a phone call where my ex was clearly relieved to get rid of me. One in which this ex did not even have the decency to meet me face-to-face if only to inform me of the impending fate of our relationship of half a decade. Thinking back to that evening, my ex had been one of the first ones, perhaps, to indulge in the art of ghosting, albeit partially.

So yes, food was important that evening. I still remember mouthing spoonfuls of rice while staring up at the ceiling, philosophizing the meaning and purpose of life itself, of love, affection, most importantly, trust. My trust shaken to its very roots, I was somehow holding up, willing myself not to shatter into bits. I told myself I was doing alright.

"You're going to survive this. It's just a stupid break-up!" I kept repeating as my woeful brain was throwing up one sweet memory after another, similar to how you'd puke slugs non-stop if you were a student at Hogwarts and someone had slapped you with a slug-vomiting spell.

"Focus on the chicken curry!" my survival instinct barked at me from somewhere inside my gut. Or it could have been my brain masquerading as my gut. I listened to it, and the universe seemed somewhat bearable after that. In fact, I must have eaten to my heart's content to quell the pain.

Things to note if you have or are about to be in a break-up for no fault of yours:

1) Inevitably, your brain will turn into a super-brain and bring forth all those images and memories of your ex that hurt the most. It will start with the day you met her/him, the moment he/ she smiled at you, and a soft sigh of 'I wish...' had escaped you, like an inflated balloon losing some of its air.

2) Much to your annoyance, your television will have conspired with your brain and will churn out romantic movies and sitcoms; ones that you once loved. But now, they will pierce your heart and sanity like spiteful, poisoned arrows. Flipping channels will not help much and you'll need guts of steel to turn that thing off.

3) If you are anything like me, you'll cry. Remember that crying is your body's most natural and inexpensive go-to for pain relief. It is actually wonderful to cry after a heartbreak. Heavy showers bring clear, sunny skies. No one reminded me of that (because I was alone at home that evening), but I'm here to remind you.

I didn't cry myself to sleep that night, but I recall staying awake until the wee hours, just staring at the walls, willing the room to dissolve into nothingness. It stayed the same, thankfully. My restlessness caused me to finish a large bag of very greasy chips and all that salt made my throat hurt. I had the sniffles after such a lengthy crying fit. When my mom called to check on me, I disconnected the call and messaged her 'Goodnight.'

I disconnected from the entire world that night. Spent and trapped in my head, I lamented my loss and bristled with rage alternately. Until sleep took me under its merciful wings.

A dreamless, disturbed sleep. I woke up abruptly, baying for blood. I decided to call him and tell him exactly what I thought of him! Bad move.

Initially, his voice seemed excited to have received my call, but as I rattled off, his tone morphed into a crisp, dry, business-like version.

That is to be expected. My ex announced he had a meeting and could I call back later. I did. The call went unanswered. I left it at that.

He returned my call one and a half years later. He said he could not get me out of his (*inflated*) head (*here I pictured myself squatting inside his squiggly brain, a very unflattering vision*) and would I meet him that evening to reminisce about our old times together. I understood he was married and in town.

Breezily, I told him I'd be at a particular spot at 6 p.m. I didn't go. I went to get ice cream.

Some bad days become unforgettable. I didn't get any ice cream that day. I had forgotten my wallet!

-Joyeeta N. Chowdhury

The Surprised 25th Anniversary

I LOVE PARTIES THROWN in my honor, even if they're surprise parties (as long as someone discreetly steers me to the appropriate wardrobe choice). In particular, I look forward to milestone birthday and anniversary parties.

It was a warm sunny June in Northern Ontario. Not only was our daughter graduating from high school, but the week before her big day, my husband and I were celebrating our 25th wedding anniversary. On the evening of our anniversary, we went out for supper, alone, at our favorite restaurant. We were a bit suspicious, as it was quite unlike our family and friends to let this milestone pass with no fanfare. Our daughter noticed our confusion and assured us we would do something the following week; once our son arrived home from London, Ontario, for her graduation. We weren't sure what this meant, and something about her demeanor told us not to make additional inquiries.

Three days before her graduation, my husband flew to a convention in Calgary. He would fly home, connecting via Toronto, the afternoon before the grad. Our worried daughter made him promise he would not miss it. He assured her he would be back in plenty of time, which seemed an easy promise to honor until the day he was to leave Calgary. Toronto started experiencing severe thunderstorms that morning; with forecasts for unsettled weather throughout the day.

As a frequent flyer, I knew this type of weather wreaked havoc with flight schedules and resulted in more broken promises than my teenager vowing to clean her room. As the day wore on, I wore out the computer keyboard checking my husband's flight status. I became more and more doubtful that he would make it to Toronto that day, let alone get on one of the very few connecting flights to Northern Ontario. Even if he made it into Toronto and stayed overnight, the chances of him getting home in time for the morning grad ceremony were slim. My daughter was becoming more anxious by the minute; and my son, who had flown home without event the day before, was pacing, a habit uncustomary for my normally undisturbed firstborn.

That evening, my son would go to my aunt and uncle's house for a visit. My daughter, the chair of her grad committee, left the house before dinner with files in hand. She was handing over the baton to her successor to ensure a smooth transition for the following year's graduation activities. I thought she might be a bit overdressed, but she made a casual comment that the girls were celebrating a night out as well.

As the time for my son to leave approached, my aunt called and invited me to go over as well. My first instinct was to decline. I was up to my elbows stripping meat off a ham bone, to prepare for the cold buffet I would serve up at my house for the big grad party the following day. I also didn't want to leave the house until I had an update from my husband (cell phones were not so common back then). I received the long-awaited phone call from my husband. He assured me he had landed in Toronto and was renting a car to drive the eight hours home through the night. The only option at this point to keep his promise to our daughter. After his assurances and much cajoling from my son, I removed my food-stained apron, changed into something I hoped didn't smell like ham, and went with my son.

I had a strange feeling about this whole thing. My suspicions were confirmed when we arrived at my aunt and uncle's front door and a houseful of guests yelled, "Surprise!!!!"

The first thing that crossed my mind was the irrational thought that perhaps my husband was there, and this was part of the whole surprise. My first words were, "Is Rob here?" My rational side reminded me how ludicrous this was because why would he surprise me at our 25th-anniversary party? I didn't know if there was a precedent for a groomless celebration. But my family, who subscribed to the "no party poopers allowed" rule, handed me a glass of wine and we celebrated just the same. I posed for pictures with my stand-in groom, a mantel-sized statue of Michelangelo's David, watched the beautiful slideshow the kids put together, and listened to my son recite a funny and heartfelt poem he and my daughter had written. I held back tears and smiled through it all, knowing that my husband would have been so touched, and dreaded when I had to tell him what he missed.

Someone had the brilliant idea that we should save the cake and decorations for the following day. The guest list was almost the same anyway, and we could combine the grad party and the 25th anniversary all into one celebration. My husband arrived home at 4 a.m., and we said nothing to him until the grad party was in full swing that afternoon. My cousin lured him outside to show off his new vehicle while we quickly switched decorations, brought the cake out of hiding, and set up the slideshow. I signaled to my cousin to end the ruse, he ushered my husband back in and we all yelled, "Surprise!!!"

It was very confusing for my bleary-eyed, sleep-deprived husband, who continued to have many questions even after being briefed about the first surprise party, eating cake, and toasting many more years of wedded bliss.

For all my love of celebrations, I guess I ended up with two, or perhaps more like one and a half. We refer to the first one (groom-less) as my 25th-Anniversary party and the second one as ours.

-Norma Gardner

You Can't Die of Embarrassment. I Know. I Tried.

I N LATE OCTOBER 1993, my husband and I checked into the newly opened *Treasure Island Hotel and Casino* in Las Vegas for the wedding of my husband's colleague. Even late in the year, outdoor temperatures can be brutal. We dressed in our wedding finery for the midday service and crossed the steaming black road to a little chapel. I had chosen a pink suit, white nylon shell, white tights, and black, flat Mary Janes. The fabric under my armpits dampened. I'd have to keep the jacket on to mask the dark circles.

The shoes were a compromise. Foot trouble forced me to wear them, and I did so only with reluctance. I'm short and usually wear heels to compensate. In flats, I was self-conscious of my height. I can't change it, but I can feel a hefty dose of embarrassment, especially in crowds. In my fantasy world, all my troubles would vanish by being five inches taller. My younger sister is mistaken for older because she towers over me. To say I feel frustrated about my lack of stature would be a massive understatement. Resentment. Vexation. Exasperation.

The return slog was even worse. The brilliant sun beat down on our heads and it felt like my scalp would burst into flames at any second. I couldn't wait to get into the cool, air-conditioned comfort of the casino. Along with all the other overdressed participants, envious of the gamblers in their sun wear, we trouped through the main casino to the reception deep in the bowels of the resort. It was strangely quiet down there. Canned music echoed off the walls. The heat seemed to have sapped any conversation.

Inside the ballroom, under soaring ceilings and crystal chandeliers, we headed to our designated table. Once seated, I felt more comfortable. From the waist up, I'm on par with most women, statuesque goddesses notwithstanding.

Then we all waited for the wedding couple to appear. Waiters delivered cold beverages and the mood in the room lifted. We chatted, sipped cocktails, and waited. And waited. Eventually, I couldn't hold off a trip to the bathroom. It turned out our table was far from the exit, but I doubt anyone noticed me leave. People's gaze didn't gravitate to short individuals. At that moment, I felt grateful for my invisibility.

Compared to the increasing volume of conversation in the ballroom, the hall was silent. I did my business and headed back. Standing in the hall in front of the entrance that led inside, I could hear soft pop music from hidden speakers in the corridor. I eased open the door to sneak back in, hoping the evening would move on at a better pace. One can only smile politely for so long before cheek muscles begin to spasm.

I slid into the ballroom. *Blue Suede Shoes* began blaring over the sound system, and the glare of a spotlight landed on me. I squinted in the light, but not before I witnessed everyone in the room, all two hundred or so, turn to stare at me. And laugh. Mortified, heat flushed my cheeks, and my gaze dropped to my white legs and black shoes. *Why had I worn those stupid flats? And white tights? Why can't I grow a few inches?* I must have looked like a cartoon character, pink, white, and round.

I felt myself melting even shorter than the Wicked Witch of the West in *The Wizard of Oz*. Panic gripped me and forced breath from my lungs. There was nowhere to hide. I couldn't just leave and go back to our hotel room, though that was exactly what I wanted to do. I lowered my head and made for the table and my husband. He told me he felt powerless to help, but he also didn't understand my unease at being so short. Thinks it's cute. At almost six feet tall, it's not something he's ever had to live with.

He also shared that they had been expecting an Elvis impersonator. I had already stolen Elvis' thunder when he showed up a few minutes later from a different door. To this day, I wear heels to weddings, and I've accepted I have a bigger chance of shrinking even shorter than growing taller. With that acceptance has come some peace. Now, if the spotlight finds me, I can dance a little soft shoe and end with a flourished "ta-da!"

-L. G. Reed

Booby Prize

COCKROACHES. DIESEL FUMES. No clean clothes. A week wedged into a tiny boat under a blistering sun. The honeymoon of our dreams.

Wind back twelve hours. I realized at 4 a.m. that I should have researched before agreeing to my adventurous fiancée's honeymoon destination. I had just opened her guide to Ecuador and The Galapagos Islands. What else can you do when jet lag has left you wide awake in airport limbo six thousand miles from home? With just a fanny pack.

"Don't come if you're going to spend the week wondering why you've flown thousands of miles to sit on a burning rock watching a few birds in the searing sun," began the guidebook introduction. Oh, dear.

Ecuador's capital, Quito, was our penultimate stop. Airline staff eventually escorted me and my wife, along with a crowd of other dazed passengers, to a vast hangar. We all shuffled between endless rows of suitcases and rucksacks, occasionally flipping over a luggage tag to pretend we hadn't given up being reunited with our belongings.

My wife and I were due to spend the night in a downtown hotel before our onward flight to the Galapagos Islands. However, the delayed arrival of our flight, coupled with our fruitless hunt for our luggage, had upset our plans. Both of our frame rucksacks had clearly read the guidebook and jetted off to their own more interesting honeymoon destination.

Commercial services had apparently expanded a little on the Galapagos Islands since their first "post office" - a wooden barrel used as a post box - appeared in 1793. Even two centuries later, however, shopping while touring the mostly deserted islands wasn't really an option.

But the airline gave my wife and me fifty US dollars each to buy essentials - a small fortune given how much of the trip was already on our credit cards.

I couldn't believe how fast the digits on our beaten-up taxi's meter were spinning. Fortunately, the total came to just under a thousand sucres - the value of the one large denomination banknote I had.

When I held out the note to the driver, he lifted his hands as if to say he had no change. It did include a small tip, but I was still confused. "Muchas gracias, señor," he said, bowing his head as he took the note. Was I meant to have haggled him down?

Only when we checked into our hotel did I understand. "You gave the driver a thousand sucres for bringing you from the airport?" asked the receptionist incredulously.

"It said nine hundred and something on the meter," I replied.

"Taxis still have the old meters," she explained. "You must divide the total by ten."

Whoops. Well, at least our nine hundred percent tip had gone to a nice driver who hadn't deliberately set out to rip us off.

Ordinarily, we might have asked the hotel to swap our twin-bedded room for one with a double bed. This was the first night of our honeymoon, after all. But it was no longer a priority as we didn't dare fall asleep because missing our Galapagos plane would mean missing our boat.

After a "night" so short and devoid of sleep that describing it as such was a flagrant misuse of the English language, we dashed into the only department store in sight, each armed with our fifty dollars. We could only see children's clothes. Till we realized that, though we are barely average height in the UK, in Ecuador we were semi-giants. So we grabbed what torso-compressing T-shirts and toe-squishing espadrilles we could and jumped into a taxi.

Just as our taxi hit Quito's quiet outskirts, we heard a loud pop. A tire had burst. The driver ushered us out of the car. Traffic hurtled past but there were no other taxis.

The driver frantically pushed his open palms in our direction. We took this to mean that our best chance of living to tell this tale was to stand well away from the road. He rummaged around in his boot and removed a rusty jack and an even rustier tire iron. Our watch wrists had never experienced so much movement.

Miraculously, we were soon back on the road, our taxi now shod with a worryingly bald spare wheel. Time was ridiculously tight. As money would be if we had to spend the week in Quito since we'd paid upfront for the week-long Galapagos trip.

Fortunately, there was a blip in our run of bad luck. Our next plane had been delayed, so we could board after all and fly into San Cristobal airport. We met our guide, and a pickup took us to our boat.

The crew made sympathetic noises after the guide explained why my wife and I had no luggage. The captain said that, though our package did not include dessert, he would make an exception for our first lunch on board. It seemed the less you paid, the more rice you ate. Doubtless, the tourists on the big ships sat down to multiple courses washed down with wine of their choosing. We, meanwhile, sat down to a single plate of rice with minute slivers of whitish fish. And water in a child's plastic beaker.

But at least today, thanks to all the first world problems we'd endured, we would get a postre - dessert. Like anyone with a sweet tooth, I have my favorites. Would it be cheesecake? Chocolate mousse? Apple pie? I'd even be fine with vanilla ice cream. And the dessert was... red jello. I don't know about where you live, but in the UK, jello is most commonly served up at birthday parties... until the age of five.

Worse was to come. After our late lunch on board, I'd lain down to nap under a deck canopy as protection from the afternoon sun. Except my feet stuck out, my ankles turned crimson, and my tight espadrilles began feeling even tighter. Every step was agony. I tried my bunk only to discover that a family of cockroaches had booked onto the same tour; while every breath I took seemed infused with gasoline fumes from the boat's engine.

At least the ammonia-filled air that shot up my nostrils when we stepped onto our first island made a change from the stench of the engine. That's when I spotted my first blue-footed booby. And my second. And my third. Because the Galapagos islands are so isolated, the birds did not fear predators. My shipmates and I were practically standing over them. Their large, webbed feet looked like they'd been soaked in the bright paint of "blue" cities' architecture: Santorini, Greece or Jodhpur, India.

The boobies' soft, downy necks looked eminently strokable as each male made a huge point of lifting each sky-blue foot in turn to woo every potential mate. Then he outstretched his wings to every conceivable angle in case the female hadn't yet appreciated just what a catch he was. Finally, he clacked his long dark beak to show he wanted to be more than just friends. The males appeared to be taking themselves so seriously as they performed their antics that I couldn't help but do the opposite. The week was going to be more enjoyable than I'd anticipated.

Oh, and unlike most blue-footed booby pairings, my wife and I are still together.

-*Tony Elston*

Shame on You, Not Me

I RECENTLY STARTED A blog about my disastrous dating life and now that I feel a tad more secure about it, I am sharing it with more friends, and even past dates. "Do not worry," I tell an ex-suitor over the phone. "We went out way before the blog's timeline, your story will not show up."

He responded all smooth and what not, "We must fix that immediately and date again." I got a little flustered. Have I mentioned that I am a sucker for words? He continued, "There is nothing to hide, mi amor. I have always been a gentleman; you can write anything you want about me."

It is wonderful that we were not having this conversation in person, so he could not see my jaw drop. I am thankful to my dentist and his fabulous skills, considering my new implant was on full display. "You stood me up, Jerk!" I wanted to scream.

Never Showed Up Guy went on reciting his attributes and why it is okay for me to include him in the blog. To be fair, I had not seen him (except for Facebook) since he was a boy. I do not know the man he is today. We had one date, back when I started college in Massachusetts and was often traveling back home to Puerto Rico. Mami was in a brand-new soap opera (she is an actress) and he played her son (he is an actor). I met him at the television studio, he asked me out, and with giddy enthusiasm, I accepted what would be my first "real" date.

Never Showed Up Guy picked me up in a fancy car (probably his dad's but who cares?), complimented my outfit, opened the car door for me, and took me to a trendy place to eat and dance; the whole nine yards of seduction. I got my first public kiss on that dance floor. Embarrassed by the public display of affection, I rapidly looked down when the kiss ended. He gently lifted my chin with his hand and whispered, "Never be embarrassed of anything you do." There is still a Marta-shaped puddle in that ballroom at the Cerromar. At the end of the night, when asked for a second date, I softly said yes with whatever I had left of my voice.

I am still waiting for him to pick me up for that second date.

I remember sitting on the bed in my childhood room, wearing a bright orange parachute long shirt (it was the 80s; be kind), black leggings, and orange flats. My sisters and Mami kept coming in and out of my room while I waited. They looked so sad. After the time of his expected arrival passed, and passed, and passed, Mami sat next to me. Caressing my hair in that way she does, which makes everything right again. She said with kindness, "Hija mia, he is not going to show up. It is his loss. One day, he will look back on this day and realize what a fool he is." I held on to Mami and sobbed; the pain of my young, inexperienced heart so deep it felt as if I would cry forever. I was full of shame. And it hurt.

That was the only time I have ever been stood up. Ever.

Never Showed Up Guy's conversation was still happening on the other end of the phone. I interrupted and exclaimed with joy, "Yes! What a fantastic idea! Let's go out again! I will pick you up tonight at 7 p.m. What is your address? Wait for me; I will be there. I promise."

'Heaven has no rage like love to hatred turned, nor hell a fury like a woman scorned.'

-Marta A Oppenheimer

That Wasn't in the Plans

G ROWING UP, I WASN'T the girl who dreamed about getting engaged or my future proposal. I didn't care what my future ring looked like, if the boy got down on one knee, or even how it happened.

I wasn't against getting married, but my focus was always on other things. It would be exciting once it happened, but until that time, it didn't merit my thoughts.

Fast forward to the time of my life when many of those close to me were getting engaged; I still didn't have plans for what I wanted, but I had cynically created a list of things I *didn't* want.

I didn't want to be surprised. Didn't want to be proposed to in public or around other people. No cheesy speech (I have a bad habit of laughing in those situations). And most of all, there was this *one* restaurant and this *one* beautiful place that if a boyfriend even considered proposing at; I would say no automatically, because obviously he didn't know me at all.

Fast forward again to the time I was finally dreaming about my proposal. I knew it was coming. My boyfriend had the ring and had already gotten approval from my father. But the biggest tell was that *he* made plans for us to go on a date.

It was a Friday evening when he came and picked me up for our date.

I was finally *that* girl. I was excited and dreaming of what our night would be like.

He took me to our favorite restaurant for special occasions. I was inwardly patting him on the back for his smart choice.

We walked past the crowd to get our reserved table... to be told they accidentally double-booked the reservation. Since the other party arrived earlier, they didn't have a table for us. We could wait, but it would be a couple of hours before a table would open.

Bummed out, we went back to our car to decide on a different restaurant. There was a lot around. We would make it work.

Only it was a Friday night and what we found was long wait time... after long wait time. It came down to two choices. Fast Food or *that one* restaurant. My boyfriend decided on *that one* restaurant.

I inwardly cringed and panicked. *What if he ends up proposing there? I have vowed to never accept a proposal at that place. Is he testing me? They better have their Crème brûlée tonight...*

We made it to the restaurant, and I grabbed a Crème brûlée from the buffet on the way to our table. Although I never wanted *this* place to be a part of my proposal, that didn't mean I would not eat my share and enjoy every last bite.

My boyfriend decided since our plans derailed to have some fun with me. He would keep pausing and dramatically say, "I have something to tell you.... I like this ham." Or romantically grab my hand. "I have a question for you—long drawn-out pause with eye contact—would you... like me to get you more Crème brûlée?"

At this point, I didn't care how much I loved him. If he asked me to marry him right then, the answer was no.

Full and satisfied, we left the restaurant well-fed and NOT engaged.

Of course, to my dismay, after going to that *one* restaurant, we took a walk through that *one* beautiful place, which just happened to be right next door.

It was beautiful. Full of couples in love. And a romantic atmosphere. I knew it hadn't been in my boyfriend's plans, but when he kneeled to tie his shoe (that was already tied), I ran away. He would not get the satisfaction of playing another joke on me.

Acting mock offended that I ran from him, we headed off to the next portion of the grand plan. Ice skating at an outdoor rink. A place I loved and that held happy memories for us. I was super excited. It was coming. Hopefully, he would ask me privately and wouldn't give some big, orchestrated speech in front of the crowds.

Only when we arrived, we found the rink closed to the public for a private event.

We laughed and joked about how nothing ever goes to plan, then decided to head home.

It has been a fun night, even with all the chaos.

As we got close to my house, I pondered the level of my disappointment. It wasn't like we wouldn't still end up engaged and married at some point, but I had really looked forward to it happening that night.... Suddenly, my boyfriend took a wrong turn.

Wait!? We aren't going home yet.

Instead of taking me home, my boyfriend took me to "my favorite place in the world". A small area at the base of the canyon near my home. I had taken him there once before and explained how I would frequently visit this place. Happy or sad, it was the place I would go to be alone. My little piece of heaven.

As we pulled into the parking area, I found it hard to stay calm. I was inwardly patting his back again and squealing with joy.

We walked around for a bit, marveling at the beauty and glory of nature during the fall and the many stars present on that dark, cloudless night.

It was absolutely perfect. And it was finally here!

My boyfriend paused and got down on one knee. He pulled out a box, opening it to display a beautiful ring with the moonlight glowing within it. Clearing his throat, he asked, "Will you marry me—

When out of the bushes, right behind him, glowing eyes grew bigger and bigger. Getting closer and closer. Then out of the bushes crept a giant raccoon.

I screamed. And screamed some more. Then I ran. Straight to the car where I immediately jumped in.

Shaking in my seat, my boyfriend joined me a minute later.

Laughing, he looked at me. "So..."

"So what?"

"So, do you want the ring?"

It was my turn to laugh as I grabbed the ring from him and put it on my finger.

Chuckling, he started driving away.

The night was everything I had *never* dreamed of and more.

-Amilee Weaver Selfridge

Definitely Not a Bridezilla

M Y ELDEST DAUGHTER, REBECCA, celebrated her marriage amid a series of unfortunate mishaps.

Shortly before the wedding, her photographer became ill leaving us without a replacement until the night before the wedding. I couldn't believe it was all happening as three weeks earlier, she discovered the dress she was to wear didn't fit. Off we went to buy material and find a pattern, whilst searching for a seamstress. A talented lady, called Joy, did a remarkable job, finishing a new one in two and a half weeks.

On the day of the wedding, the bridal car broke down, not once, but twice. They were using, the groom's, customized Ford Falcon. I knew we shouldn't have, knew something would become amiss. The second time we were in the wrong car park, at Werribee Gardens, where the wedding was to be performed. We walked almost a quarter of a kilometer (270 yards) through the grounds, to find the rest of our wedding party and guests.

We were already over half an hour late. They sent me ahead with their wedding rings jammed on my fingers, phone, and video camera thrust at me, to hurry forward to alert the guests we were finally there. Stockings ripped from stumbling along, which fortunately no guests noticed. Smiling my apologies, I handed over the rings to the best man and assured, Wayne, her fiancé, all was well.

The little flower girl, Mackenzie, had refused to carry the pillow with the rings and instead had pulled some fake flowers from a vase at home, insisting she carry her own bouquet. She was also tired, and Rebecca had to carry her through the grounds, in her wedding dress, before handing her over to her father.

None of this fazed Rebecca. She just brushed down her dress, flicking off some dirt and dust from the little girls' shoes, and continued on. She looked radiant and relaxed as she walked towards Wayne, who was waiting anxiously for her arrival.

My beautiful mother, who unfortunately has Alzheimer's, was sitting next to me, totally oblivious to what was going on, trying to point out things in the gardens and chatting animatedly. Keeping her quiet meant I missed out on most of the wedding vows. Thank goodness for video cameras, which captured what I missed. After having family photos taken, I rushed off to the function center to make sure all was in order. You can imagine my horror when I arrived at 5:15 to see none of the tables set and our food and drinks, not in our cool room. With our guests due to arrive in fifteen minutes, we literally threw the cutlery on the tables. Some guests were wonderful, helping to carry the drinks through the function center, to where they belonged.

Fortunately, Rebecca and Wayne, were oblivious to all this, as they were still having their photos taken.

I had strict instructions from my youngest daughter, Elizabeth, who decorated the cake, on how to arrange it on the table. We were running so late it literally got thrown together on its tiers and fortunately... looked perfect to me.

I held my breath, as the happy couple made a fabulous grand entrance, car diving through sliding doors and into the function room. Thankfully the brakes on Wayne's car didn't fail. Fortunately, all was well and they alighted without a hitch. Ambulances rushing off to ferry the injured guests to the hospital would have been too much for me to bear.

The woman hired to do the dishes did not clear the tables, so Rebecca, still in her wedding dress, and I, with the help of some very dear friends, did so as we chatted with the guests at each table.

The girl hired to look after the bar fell ill and left early, leaving me and two of my very dearest friends, to clear up and wash glasses. I, in my expensive "mother of the bride outfit" washed dishes until midnight.

Kathryn, my second daughter, kicked off her shoes, hoisted up her bridesmaid's dress, and threw herself into cleaning. Elizabeth plowed in as well, packing up the car with gifts and left-over food and drink. Unfortunately, I never had a chance to welcome our guests or to thank them on their departure for coming to share in this wonderful day.

Rebecca, to her credit, did not once complain. Most brides would have been crying or throwing some sort of tantrum. After packing up our cars, we arrived back at their home, no expensive honeymoon suite for these two, and watched all that I missed on their video camera.

The funniest bit at the end of the night was when Rebecca and Wayne were seeing off their guests; and there I was, in the background, with my friends, loading and ferrying it off to the kitchen.

It must have looked like a comedy sketch and we certainly laugh about it now.

It was still a wonderful night. The most rewarding part was receiving messages from friends who thought the night was fantastic and commented on how well we'd organized it all.

If only they knew!

-Deva Shore

I'VE BEEN ON ROLLER-COASTERS SMOOTHER THAN THAT...

It was sure lucky running into you, Dad!
I'm going to need cab fare!

Road Rage

I T WAS A MONDAY morning, and when I awoke, I noticed that the sun was already up. In my groggy state, it took me a few minutes to realize that this was not normal. I usually get up for work around 5:00, and it is dark at that time. As soon as it hit me that the sun's welcoming was out of place, I grabbed my phone to look at the time. 7:00! I was going to be late!

My morning routine is ritualistic. I get up early so that I can have plenty of time to drink my coffee and mentally prepare myself for the day. Oversleeping meant that not only would I not get my coffee, but I wouldn't get breakfast or a shower either.

I went into action. A bird bath replaced my usual shower, and I grabbed a diet soda and a pack of crackers on my way out the door. Down the road I went, focused on one mission: not being late for work. Not fully awake, I ran a red light. I immediately realized what I had done, but as I surveyed the scene, I saw I had luckily caused no accidents. The only effect of my traffic violation was that I cut someone off.

Phew! That could have been bad.

Since I saw no major consequences from my driving error, I continued down the road. As I did, a car zoomed past me, and then stopped right in front of me, blocking both lanes of traffic. I slammed on my brakes and stared through still-sleepy eyes. A woman jumped out of her car and started heading toward me. As I regained my focus, I noticed she was the one that I accidentally cut off when I ran the red light.

Since she blocked me in, I couldn't drive off, so I had no choice but to sit there and await this lady's wrath. She approached my car, and I locked my door but cracked my window so that we could communicate. What I saw next was a rage that was extremely hyperbolic for what had occurred. I made a simple traffic mistake, but from this woman's reaction, I might have been the first person on earth to do so.

Her reaction was so absurd, in fact, that I actually questioned whether I was even awake. Maybe I didn't oversleep, and the whole bad morning was a dream. I sat there speechless while she ranted on, questioning whether I would wake up and start a normal day equipped with coffee, a shower, and breakfast.

For what seemed like several minutes, I sat in silence, and this mad woman filled the silence with intense words of rage. When I finally snapped out of my daze, the absurdity of what was happening added to the morning I had already had. And I started laughing! Not just a mumbled giggle, but a full-blown hysterical laugh. In a split second, our roles reversed: my new foe became silent, and I was suddenly the crazy woman, laughing uncontrollably.

This may have been the only reaction I could have had that would ease her anger. Shocked, she stared at me for a few seconds, then shook her head and walked back to her car. She stomped to my car, prepared to fight, but when my laugh was as out of place as her screaming, she didn't know how to react.

I gathered my composure and proceeded to work. Amazingly, the rest of the day went quite smoothly after I turned my bad morning around with a completely maniacal laugh.

-Tammy Brown

Turnpike Trauma

BEING THE DUTIFUL HUSBAND I am, I recently offered to drive my wife Allison from our home in New Rochelle (NY) to Newark Airport. I have always hated to drive and do so only if I absolutely must. Even though I am a "white knuckle" driver with a terrible sense of direction, I braved the George Washington Bridge and delivered her to the airport myself.

Trying to ease my discomfort behind the wheel, Allison drove us to the airport. Pointing out landmarks to help guide me on the trip back.

She repeatedly told me, "When you leave the airport, don't forget, look for signs for 78 EAST." Like a cult member, I chanted it back each time. We arrived with no incident, and I began the adventure home.

I followed Allison's directions, which now came to me like a Catholic schoolboy's preaching precepts. And it worked! I made it onto the 78 EAST. Since it was midday, with barely any traffic, I expected it would take less than an hour to make it home. "Call me when you get home", Allison had instructed. "I'll probably still be waiting to board."

Less than ten minutes into my drive, I was only a hundred yards from the Turnpike toll booth when — pop! Then the unmistakable thump of a flat tire. Scratching sounds drowned out my cursing as the metal rims hit the highway. Come on, I can make it to the median strip. I stopped in the strip between the two lanes of traffic and pondered what I should do. Getting out of the car was clearly not an option. Given the traffic rocketing past me, I was likely to become a human pancake before making it to the side of the road.

Changing the tire was hopeless, but I did know how to call AAA. While watching the cars whiz by me, I was told repeatedly how important my call was.... An AAA representative finally came on but told me the Turnpike was in New Jersey Turnpike Authority domain, not theirs. But she would notify the Authority of my problem and send them along soon. Thirty minutes later, there they were. I jumped out of my car to meet them.

"Stay in your car!"

Chastened, I got back in the car while the repairman changed the tire.

"This spare will not get you home."

After getting directions to a used tire shop in Jersey, only two exits away, I headed off. Until—pop. There went the spare tire.

I wondered if you could cry and drive at the same time?

Riding the rim to the next exit, I pulled into the parking lot of another toll plaza. At least being off the highway, I could get out of the car. I called AAA again, figuring since I was no longer on the highway, they should be able to help me. Wrong! The Turnpike Authority oversees the toll plaza too. And if I wait, this time they will send a flatbed truck.

Allison was boarding soon, and I had a choice to make. I could call now—and have her worry about how I am going to get myself out of this mess. Or wait to call—and have her worry the entire plane ride about what has happened to me.

I called. Allison seemed concerned, but thankfully with the plane about to take off, we had to cut the conversation short. After my best "there's nothing to worry about" performance, she said she wouldn't worry.

When the tow truck finally came, they loaded my car onto the flatbed and brought it to the garage they assured would fix me up with a tire. They offloaded my car, with me still in it, onto the street in front of the garage. My automotive problems were close to being solved!

I waited for my car in a small, grubby room, with motor oil posters and a calendar from 2015. When I checked my phone, I found two voicemails. The first is from Allison's business associate, Linda. I can't imagine why she called me. Turns out, Allison asked her to check on me, then let her know I was okay. So much for my plans to keep her from worrying! The other voicemail, my office manager, was a wellness check finding out why I didn't return two hours ago as planned. I don't know what they would have done if something happened to me, but it was a nice thought. I returned both calls and assured everyone I was safe and would be home soon.

After some time, the mechanic finally put a full-size tire on the car. I was so paranoid about another tire blowing out that I bought an extra tire to throw in the trunk as well.

At long last, I was feeling optimistic and ready to go home. The big Route 78 letters marked the entrance to the highway, a mere fifty feet from the shop. I started driving. Only, I realized I should have been driving toward the George Washington Bridge, but...I was driving away from it. Again—I got off the turnpike.

After a consult with Google Maps, I drove around Jersey City for 20 minutes before turning into what seemed to be a dead-end. But was actually the entrance to Route 78—EAST. Now I simply had to drive through rush hour. Given how my day had gone, I was anxious another mishap would befall me before I made it home. But I arrived, with my full car still intact, back to our apartment building in New Rochelle.

Before leaving the garage, I looked back at my Toyota and muttered, "I hope you're happy here, cause I'm not moving you again, ever."

-Ed Friedman

Wrecks, Screwdrivers, and Rainbows

M Y DAUGHTER HAD JUST gotten her driver's license and wanted to drive alone for the very first time to go pick up an $11 paycheck from a restaurant. I didn't feel right about it but had no credible excuse, so I gave her the keys. An hour and a half later, I realized she had been gone for too long and called her cell phone. "Where are you?"

"I went to Target to spend this enormous paycheck. In the parking lot and heading back now." So, I launched into a rant about the dangers of driving and talking on a cell phone when my daughter interrupted me— "I just got into a wreck!"

How? There weren't any loud noises. She must have been joking. She wasn't. Immediately I left for Target and arrived long before the police. The car was in the middle of an intersection, wounded badly. A woman, who was not looking at the road, drove her big SUV into the passenger's side door of my daughter's car. She was standing with my daughter and a gentleman who witnessed the accident. This woman started yelling, arms waving wildly above her head, fists closed. Then, she started forward toward my daughter. I got between them and calmly announced to this crazed woman that I owned the car, and she was dealing with ME. The gentleman/witness suggested gently that the woman go wait close to her vehicle, which had no obvious damage. The police eventually came and made a lengthy investigation. But gave nobody a ticket, saying the insurance company could decide who was at fault, as both of us were with the same company.

So, we headed home at long last. My daughter was so shaken she said she could not drive home, or ever again. I couldn't drive two cars, so there was no other choice. We went slowly and carefully with her following me and finally made it back to our driveway. All in all, a very bad evening, but we were relieved to be home now that the hour was getting late, and the stress exhausting. We started to go inside when I noticed the dome light in the car was still on. Upon inspection, the passenger door caved in so badly that the sensor thought the door was open and kept the light on. Well, that would burn the battery down, so we couldn't leave it. We asked a neighbor for help, but he was getting on in years and was not able to. My daughter said it was all too much for her and that she was going to throw up. Always one with a sensitive digestive system, I was not surprised but told her to come right back as we had to solve this problem. "How?" she asked. I didn't know. I had no ideas and no knowledge in this area. I was losing all hope—then I saw it. In the floorboard, almost under the driver's seat, was my father's screwdriver! It had been around forever. I remember being preschool-age and watching my father work on things with it, occasionally being asked to hand it to him. I grabbed it up quickly and showed it to her as the idea entered my mind. "With this!"

I unscrewed the cover on the dome light and used it to pry the bulb out. I was breathing a sigh of relief when I realized the problem still wasn't solved. A small light under the dash, that we had never even noticed, was still on. It was hard to get to and I couldn't reach it. My daughter became empowered. She took the screwdriver, fit into the tight space by hanging upside down, and while I shone the flashlight down on her—she fixed it. We solved our problems with the inspiration from my father's screwdriver. The screwdriver was like a rainbow after a storm, and I had no idea why it was even in the car.

The insurance company ended up denying my claim and the other driver's claim against me. The passenger door never opened again.

-Mary Traynham

Stop and Go

M Y RACING TEAM COMPRISED a group of Cape Canaveral rocket engineers who also drove sports cars. As we lived and worked in Brevard County, Florida, and all had a goofy sense of humor, the team's name naturally became "Brevard Auto Racing Fraternity" ... BARF. Amazingly, in 1964 BARF began running one of the premier endurance racing cars in the world, a Ferrari 250 GTO.

GTOs—or at least mine, chassis # 3223 GT—were not set up for big drivers. The seat, bolted in place, wasn't adjustable; and the steering column was at a low angle, pushing the bottom of the large wheel snugly over the driver's thighs. This was a challenge for taller drivers; with so little space to rotate one's right leg, it took a gymnast to do a common "heel-and-toe" downshift maneuver.

BARF's solution was to weld a small tab to the accelerator pedal. This let the driver do the trick, pointing his toe on the brake pedal and pumping his heel straight down on that tab to blip the engine revs. It was easy and effective ... as long as the driver remembered to keep his heel UP during very heavy braking. Otherwise, he'd find himself trying to slow down and speed up simultaneously!

Now about shoes. During the 1960s, many drivers wore rubber-soled tennis shoes. These raised two issues. First, if they picked up the smallest amount of oil from the pit or garage floor, they could slip on the pedals—a potential disaster. Second, rubber soles also got hot enough to numb one's feet when driving for long periods; as the car's aluminum firewall, floor, and drive-shaft cover were all un-insulated.

The recommended style was a light-weight leather-soled loafer, with a low heel or none at all. (Note that modern Nomex-lined fire-resistant shoes did not exist.) Professional drivers could find custom driving shoes in Europe, but a reasonable substitute was high-quality, snug-fitting loafers, taped over the instep to prevent them from slipping off ... another latent disaster.

In March 1966, we had very warm weather in Sebring, FL. Conditions for the 12-hour race were blazing. Jack, one of our drivers, quickly developed problems with his rubber-soled shoes during practice. As predicted, they were slippery, and the heat made his foot pain intolerable.

The crew's advice was, "Hey, Jack, switch to your leather shoes and we'll pull the heels off." But Jack had a huge objection to this idea. His high-class Gucci loafers were his favorite casual footwear. He wasn't about to tear them apart or wrap them with nasty duct tape just for a little old race.

But as practice wore on, his discomfort with the tennies rose and he experienced a few braking and shifting hiccups out on the track. So he made a concession and started wearing his precious loafers. But despite our urging, he insisted that his stylish Italian heels, about an inch high, "had to stay."

On race day, Jack, Gucci-shod, won our coin toss to be the first driver, ran the Le Mans-style starting foot race, and took off in the middle of the pack. Despite some slow laps at the beginning, he made progress during the first two hours, then pitted for service and the driver change. In those days, we only used two drivers; I jumped in, and away I went. A couple of hours later, at the second pit stop, I yelled to Jack several times, "The brakes are boiling HOT! Pedal's low until they get some cooling. Be EXTRA CAUTIOUS on the downshifts!"

Jack, excited and in a huge hurry, nodded, leaped in, zoomed away ... and six turns later, "beached" the GTO high on the sandbank at the slowest corner in endurance racing, the notorious Sebring Hairpin.

Poor guy, his fancy loafer heel betrayed him on that modified gas pedal. While downshifting from fifth gear in the Big Bend, all the way to second for that 20-mph (32-kph) Hairpin, he'd been frantically trying to STOP and GO at the same time!

Jack got out and did a walk-around. Standing by the car, he looked back up the track where he had failed to slow down enough. Cars were coming out of Big Bend and down the straight, at 150 mph (241 kph), aimed right at his soft little body. His thought was, "What if one of those guys has brake fade? Or makes the same mistake I just did? And they come charging up here on the sand WITH ME?"

Just then, no more than 300 yards (274 meters) away, a Ford GT40 catapulted high into the air and slammed down beside the track, bursting into flames. That sealed it. Jack knew his Ferrari was lightly damaged and could probably be dug out okay. But his predicament unnerved him.

We were on edge, watching from the pits as forbidding black smoke rose over the Hairpin area, and having heard the track announcer say, "Car 35 is off, in the sand."

We readied a dig-out kit—plywood slab, entrenching tool, length of rope—for me to carry to the site. (The regulations allowed one co-driver to replace a current driver and try to free a stranded car using hand-carried tools.) I was just setting out for a long hike when Jack arrived behind the pits, perched high on a wrecker beside the dented Ferrari. He had called for a tow truck; our car had been immediately DQ'd: Disqualified.

I caved in to my temper and frustration and started yelling.

"What are you DOING, Jack? I can SEE the car's bent. But it'll still run! We could bang out that fender. We were climbing the charts, man! This is stupid, Jack. Now we're out!"

Jack protested about the danger and the big crash he'd watched, but there was no good answer. The BARF crew made sure to keep us apart; after all, it was a "racing accident." They happen all the time.

The team sadly canceled its celebratory plans. Our mechanic, Gerhard, wept over how his "beautiful motor" had been wasted. Jack's brain-fade cost him a bit of a wounded ego and some extra race expenses. And that day ended one of the last international endurance races run by any Ferrari 250 GTO.

Several weeks passed before civil communications between Jack and me resumed. And there was that little matter of repair costs to be settled. The air, and the damages, were eventually cleared up, but the topic of the crash and those idiotic shoes would arise between us for many years.

Sometime later I became well acquainted with Jack's girlfriend … a delightful, stunning young woman named Seelie. She told me more of the back-story. Before the race, Jack revealed what the crew intended to do with his shoes, and Seelie had read him the riot act. It turned out the shoes were a prized personal gift, representing about a month's salary. "If you let anybody ruin those Guccis," she had told him, "you'll never get anywhere near me again."

What would you have done?

Right. That's exactly what Jack did, too.

-Larry Perkins

FLIPPING! FLYING! FILLETING?

"I'LL BE 60 THIS year—that's so old!" I mused to myself. It was just past midnight on January 1, 2006. Preoccupied with thoughts of becoming a certified senior citizen, I sped down the new 9A highway, ignoring two warning signs: Merge. Merge.

If you drive a car, you are bound to be involved in an occasional fender bender. Living in Florida, a state that brags more registered vehicles than people, it is inevitable. 400,000 annual crashes. Count me statistic 400,000 + one.

It is true. Your life does flash before when you think you are dying. My brush with the Grim Reaper prompted a personal flashback. This surreal video, better than any reality TV show, was in brilliant Technicolor. Six decades flashed through my mind as my RAV4 flipped over, over, and over. Visions of childhood antics. Teenage angst. College capers. Honeymoon passion. Workplace stress. Family adventures.

On the third flip, Little Red landed upside down in the grassy median with all her windows busted. When the Jaws-of-Life pulled me from the flattened vehicle, I was dazed and shaky, a miracle to be alive.

EMTs gently placed me on a stretcher. A Florida Highway Patrol officer interrupted, "I need to do a breathalyzer test." My groggy head faded in and out as a bitter argument escalated. "She ain't been drinking, no smell of alcohol," a young female countered as she snapped my neck restraint and security belts. An angry FHP yelled, "But it's New Year's Eve, they're all drunk tonight!" The last thing I heard was, "Then go arrest some bad guys and..."

Fade to black. I awoke to an exciting ride in the ambulance nearly as death-defying as my flipping. After an overnight stay at St. Luke's Hospital, I was released with minor cuts and bruises. Thankfully, I was not the latest rocket propelled from the Space Coast. Seatbelts and airbags rule!

Next day trip...to Bud's Auto Graveyard to bid my beloved companion, Adieu.

"Call me Buddy," an old man uttered through a semi-toothless grin. The emblem on his faded pair of overalls read B.A.G. Your Junk-Our Hunk. He led me through an unfortunate sea of crushed, mangled, and twisted vehicles. Buddy commented about the condition of the driver of each wreck: "Dead. Head trauma. Dead. Coma..." I halted his gruesome Collisions of Horror. "Where's my RAV4?"

Buddy escorted me to the rear of the junkyard. I averted my eyes from fragments of metal, plastic, and glass that were once shiny Hondas, Chevys, and BMWs. In the distance, I saw my scarlet baby. Little Red was flat, an SUV pancake. Just above the driver's side roof was a rounded arc, exactly where my head had been. "That's your halo, Little Lady," Buddy said. "It saved y'all life!"

A prophetic epiphany: last year's lover's quarrel at Arlington Toyota dealership. "Let's get the sunroof!" I cajoled.

"Forget that idea," Hubby said, "We're buying the one with the roll bar—just in case!"

Buddy spat, dribbling a line of brown juice onto his scraggly beard. Thrusting a plastic bag at me, he shouted, "What in tarnation were y'all doing with all them knives?"

In the bag were cutting implements of all sorts... a set of steak knives; knives for boning, carving, paring; saw-edged and fine-points; sharp cutters all. Then I remembered a butcher's block of cutlery, in a box, in a bag behind my car seat before the crash.

Feeling a little lightheaded, I steadied myself against the mangled fender of a used-to-be Jeep Cherokee and grabbed the bag. Tears filled my eyes, but not from crying. A baffled Buddy stared as great guffaws of snorts and giggles burst out of me. I laughed in near-convulsive hysteria at the weird headline floating through my mind's eye: "NEWS FLASH-Elderly woman survives car crash after flipping car three times. Fatality results when a meat cleaver and various sharp instruments..."

A tearful farewell to Little Red. A sincere thanks to Buddy for his help. The kindly codger gave me a high-five and smiled, "Don't y'all come back now, ya hear!" I fingered my temporary neck brace and walked gingerly through the junkyard egress.

I asked myself, "Guess what's worse than turning 60?" I muttered a prayer of thanks with the blessed insight, "Not turning 60!"

-Lucy Giardino Cortese

You Could Hardly See the Dent

L EARNING TO DRIVE WAS a liberating experience. Sitting behind the wheel, hands firmly positioned at ten and two, I was finally independent. Instead of waiting for a ride, always delayed due to misplaced car keys, I could leave when I wanted and return when I pleased.

As long as my dad didn't need the car too.

My joy in driving, at parallel parking just well enough to pass the test, was only surpassed by one feeling:

The paralyzing fear of crashing for the first time.

In my defense, it was my brother's fault. A day after I got my license, he began pestering me to drive him.

"Can we get ice cream?"

"I want to go to the basketball courts."

"I'm supposed to meet up with some friends. Can you drop me off?"

Finally, I caved. My kindness - as well as the fee I charged him - led us out onto the road and into the first of several mistakes. Not that I saw them as mistakes at the time. Cruising confidently through suburbia with my fingers splayed against the wheel and mirrors angled just right, I was the master of the road. Nevermind I was barely qualified to drive so much as a grocery store cart.

"Do I turn here?" I asked my brother, momentarily glancing over at him in the passenger's seat. With his hands gripping the armrest as I accidentally skidded against the curb - again - he looked back at me with panicked eyes.

"Yup," he replied, voice oddly high-pitched. Rolling my eyes, I continued to drive while ignoring his muttered prayers. In between me almost rolling through a red light and nearly missing a stop sign, he had suddenly become religious. I overheard him calling his girlfriend too, if his frantic, "I love you," was anything to go by. He also might have typed out his last will and testament. As stated, I would receive nothing if he perished due to my accidental vehicular manslaughter.

Honestly, the theatrics.

When we arrived, he scurried out of the car and quickly disappeared with a gaggle of his friends. Mission complete, I set out to return home. However, I quickly realized something. In dropping off my brother, I also lost my GPS. Because of my brother rushing me - clearly, the blame lies with him - I had forgotten my phone. Although I was only ten minutes away from my house, as someone who never paid attention when being chauffeured around, I was hopelessly lost. Peering out the window, a labyrinth of cookie-cutter suburban houses glared back at me. Each manicured lawn strewn with abandoned bicycles and jump ropes was, unfortunately, identical. Wonderful for preserving the monotony of suburbia. Horrible for trying to remember any identifiable landmarks to guide my way home.

Most modern teenagers, when lost and without a phone, would panic.

And that is exactly what I did.

After sobbing, my ugly blubbering having startled a judgmental dog walker or two, I considered the perilous obstacles before me. A street devoid of any cars obnoxiously parked a mile away from the curb; two lanes, with little chance of anyone driving down this way; and ample room for me to turn around and retrace my steps.

As a bonus, there were no pedestrians in sight. Along with limiting the chance I might accidentally 'love tap' someone with my car - at the snail's pace speed I still drove, a slight bump was the worst anyone would walk away from - it also eliminated any witnesses to the humiliating spectacle I was about to undertake. Slowly inching forward, I spun the wheel and grinned triumphantly when the car veered to the right.

In theory, I should have, after continuing to turn, easily found my way home along the small-town streets I had grown up on. However, theory is not reality.

In reality, I crashed into a telephone pole.

Jolting forward, my seatbelt cut into my collarbone. I fumbled with the gear shift, trying to remove the car from where it was now wedged between the curb and the wooden post. Ripping my foot off the gas, I frantically tried to back up, only to move forward again. Crying, I grabbed the steering wheel with one hand and randomly punched buttons with the other. In my haste, the windshield wipers turned on. When the car finally dislodged from the now distinctly tilted telephone post, I reversed with the newfound proficiency of a NASCAR driver and sped away.

Well, for me it was speeding. Although it's a blur, a toddler on a tricycle might have passed me, throwing a certain hand gesture too. I was too distracted by the unmistakable crunching sound the car made upon hitting the telephone post. It replayed over and over in my mind. On the drive home, I, like my brother, had a sudden revival of devoutness in the car. Praying to several deities, a few I made up myself, I wished for no one to notice the dent on the hood. For payment, I promised everything from my still-nonexistent firstborn to my stuffed animals. My willingness to part with the latter highlighted this moment of crisis.

Weaving along snaking side streets, I finally reached my undistinguishable slice of suburbia. Inhaling, I leaned against the wheel. Calmed down, I considered my options.

I could admit to my dad that I dented his car on the only obstacle along an otherwise empty street. After telling my story, and linking the true blame to my brother, I knew my dad would be disappointed. Angry, too, but mainly disappointed and reluctant to lend me his car again.

Or I could dry my eyes, take a deep breath, and go into the house pretending nothing happened. Maybe the dent wasn't as bad as I thought it sounded? Surely the panic amplified an otherwise minuscule scratch?

The first option would be difficult, but honorable. Necessary, too, if I wanted to move past this mistake.

The second option was cowardly. Sneaky. It would keep me living on a knife's edge, terrified someone might look at the car too closely.

Sighing, I exited the car and walked towards my house. It was clear what I needed to do.

Miraculously, no one immediately noticed the damage. As my mom and I left the house a few days later, with her driving and me back to my rightful status as a passenger princess, I considered if the coward's route in life was always the better one.

Until my mom suddenly stopped on the porch. Glancing at my dad's car, then back at me, she simultaneously commented and condemned me.

"Is that a dent on your dad's car?"

-Teagan Durkin

Aches, Breaks, and Big Mistakes...

It'll be a quick operation, your insurance doesn't compensate me enough for my time.

Breaking News

T HE AMBULANCE JOURNEY HAD been uncomfortable, to say
the least! Potholes you would avoid on a bike or in a car,
we seemed to target. The resulting lurch left me a screwed-up ball
of agony. It was forty miles of pain, and even worse, anticipated
pain. The excruciating thought of the next skid, bump, or round-
about was infinitely worse than the actual experience. We passed
endless suburbs of annoyingly smug bungalows. When it comes
to suburbs, I share the poet Betjeman's view. They only prolong
the journey from countryside to town!

At last, we seemed to have reached the hospital, judging by
the queues of ambulances and an indefinable sense of a general
abandonment of hope. The doors were briskly opened, and I was
slowly wheeled down the ramp, looking like a giant cocoon about
to give birth to a curious insect. I almost expected the benign
voice, David Attenborough, not the brusque, 'What's her National Health Number?'

I should go back to the beginning, which is traditionally, 'a very
good place to start'.

My trip in the ambulance, in fact, began in a convalescent home
whose sole purpose was to give succor, rest, and hope for a full
recovery. That afternoon, having given up watching the 3 o'clock
race at Sandown on TV, I painfully made my way back to my room.
The thought of doubling my problems never crossed my mind.
One painful knee replacement was more than enough. After all,
no one wants to monopolize the National Health Service with a
cycle of injuries!

I pushed the door open with one of my crutches and swung
arthritically into the room. Just as I reached for the edge of the bed,
I felt myself falling slowly backward in brilliantly executed slow
motion, worthy of any Oscar! I was lying on the floor, my head
wedged in the junction of the skirting boards, my right leg hanging

at a very odd angle, and my right foot obstinately refusing to obey orders.

An ambulance crew eventually arrived, took one look at my sprawling figure, head still wedged firmly, and pronounced it was 'more than their job's worth' to attempt to lift me!

A long time later, the fire brigade showed up. Six strong, handsome young firemen carried me down to the ambulance, like a large stuffed turkey being presented by the butler to his lordship and guests; rather more like Faulty Towers than Downton Abbey!

Back to the rather brusque receptionist. Now identified as patient number 4390621103 and transferred to a hospital trolley. They wheeled me along endless corridors with exits labeled: 'Pathology', 'Plastic Surgery', and 'Burn Unit'. After these, the 'X-ray Department' seemed almost reassuring.

Following an uncomfortable wait, a stressed Nurse broke the good news. I fractured my right hip. Luckily *it was not the same side as the knee replacement.* How little did I know the cycle was only just starting!

The next two hours remain a complete blur. Still feeling woozy and a little light-headed from the anesthesia, I was wheeled into 'Recovery'–if only all this medical terminology was true!

In the ensuing two days, I learned to avoid most of the food, to catch the eye of a nurse before a bedpan became an emergency, to ignore the strange night noises, to be ready to offer any convenient finger for a blood sample or raise an arm to check my blood pressure. All without demur, even if at two in the morning.

After three days, I was promoted/demoted to a geriatric ward. As a porter wheeled me in, I suddenly felt decidedly damp on my head and shoulders! Surely the geriatric ward wouldn't have a leak. Anyway, it hadn't rained for ages! I suddenly realized that the woman in the bed near the door had hurled a cup of tea and a glass of orange juice at me. A sort of baptismal welcome! The porter kindly wiped me down, remarking laconically that Maggie was a bit 'unpredictable'

I quickly learned the ward routine. By six in the morning, the Night Shift started waking us up. This was not difficult as most nights were disturbed with screaming, sobbing, lights on and off, trips to the bathroom, and bells summoning bedpans or commodes. Generally, it was difficult to tell night from day, except for the unvarying routine. The only 'window' at the end of the ward faced a grimy brick wall. Even at midday, there was little natural light.

The walking wounded, including myself, were perched on the edge of the bed and asked to wash in a bowl of tepid water. Admitted as an emergency, I had no belongings. 'Orphans' like myself were doomed to wear hospital gowns, the most unflattering of all garments. A shapeless piece of cloth, tied at the back with tapes, it ends up around your neck in bed and gaps embarrassingly at the back when you are walking. Here I should point out, that I have never been nominated for the 'Rear of the Year' Competition!

Breakfast and lunch passed by almost unnoticed. Supine all day, I could not face 'meat and two veg.' A meal consisting of thick slices of pork with islands of mashed potatoes and spinach, swimming in a sea of thick, brown gravy. I realized to my delight I was losing weight, a goal never reached before in the outside world.

The world of the hospital soon became the only reality. In the next bed was a tiny ninety-year-old Italian who had lost count of her many grandchildren and great-grandchildren. In the weeks I knew Maria, she seemed to shrink even further. She was a doll-like figure–tiny, fragile but still the strong Italian 'Mama'. Her many relations crowded around her bed every afternoon, paying homage with offerings of Italian treats, boxes of Tiramisu, and tubs of Panna Cotta.

Some patients, like Emily, never moved or spoke. Like waxworks in Madame Tussauds, in London, lifted in a crane-like machine into a sitting position and lowered into sleeping mode at night.

Food was spooned into their mouths and water dribbled from the corners of their lips. Visitors arrived and sat silent for a time, patted the bed, and crept guiltily away. Only on one occasion, when her daughter held up a toy dachshund, did the faintest of smiles cross Emily's face. Apparently, in that vanished world outside, she once owned a small dog.

Maggie, having given me a wet, but luckily not too warm of welcome, was at the center of most of the frantic activity in the ward. She had dementia, remembering the past in detail but totally confused by the present. Photos of her grandchildren were tucked snugly in bed beside her, their happy faces resting on the pillow. She often talked of them as her siblings, most of whom died long ago. When she became agitated and tearful, she would complain to the ward, 'This place is a prison. I'm leaving! Where's me coat and shoes?'

The portly doctor swept majestically through the ward, with his humble juniors in attendance; taking every opportunity to display the 'beautiful' incision and 'expert' stitching from when he set my fractured hip. Finally, after weeks, he pronounced me fit to be released into that other world that had become a myth, the gold at the end of the rainbow. Leaving was almost a re-birth or Second Coming, rather like emerging from a tragic film, only to be confronted by red London double-decker buses and a crowded McDonald's.

Looking back, my last view was of Maggie, a sobbing figure searching forlornly for her shoes.

I painfully swung my legs out of the scruffy taxi which had taken me to my daughter's home. I was still a novice on crutches, wobbly and insecure. Trying to remember the physio's instructions, I made slow, painful progress towards the front door. Ringing the bell was a challenge balancing on one crutch, while forlornly waving the other! I was not ready. What seemed like a pack of hounds (one elderly retriever and two Chihuahuas) rushed to greet me. Numerous children followed; arms outstretched. I fell back in graceful slow motion onto the graveled drive; surely worthy of a second Oscar?

-Sarah Elizabeth Das Gupta

Good Day Gone Bad

AFTER TWO GRUELING DAYS at the computer, I needed the sauna-warm pool that our community center provided.

"So sorry, ma'am," the Barbie-looking lifeguard humored me. "Our indoor pool is closed due to short staff. No lap lanes open now, either, in the outdoor pool."

I had not enjoyed the pleasures of an outdoor pool in years.

Being Irish and tender-skinned, the thought of back-stroking to a cloudless sun seemed risky.

How did Swim Barbie manage that pearl-like complexion?

Only a few laps, I assured myself, still wary of any rays called ultraviolet.

At the deep end, I noted two women defending their invisible lap lanes from a pack of daredevil-cannon-ballers. The more the ladies tried to reason with the boys, the more the kids enjoyed popping up and down like buoys around a boat dock.

I came over and shared my most serious teacher frown with them. Then I jumped in and commiserated in chitchat with the would-be swimmers. The boys got the hint, were polite, and found another area of the pool to have fun.

With two new friends and a clearly defined non-existent swimming lane, we proceeded to side-stroke and talk to each other. We created our own imaginary lateral lanes. Swimming in the middle of the two women, I lithely rolled from side to side to address both. I could only hope the lifeguard, who now resembled Cellphone Barbie, would appreciate my svelte water ballet.

It would be a relaxing change-of-pace day, after all.

Huddling amid noisy swimmers, we stopped swimming and treaded water to continue to chat. But several times I had to ask my new acquaintances to speak up due to my wax earplugs.

As I commented how refreshingly cool the water felt in contrast to the hot sun, I realized the earwax in my right ear felt like dripping-thin maple syrup. Self-conscious, but not letting on, I excused myself.

I swam to the pool's exit steps, placing my left foot too far into the metal ladder rung.

When I pulled my foot out of the water, I ogled a wide gash on the top of my left foot. Bright red blood streamed over my bony, high-arch.

It was safe to say I would never look at my favorite dessert, Roasted Strawberry Sundae, the same way again.

A person can endure a lot of pain in public to avoid embarrassment.

I ignored the need to limp.

I felt irritated that my left ear had a wax plug stuck snuggly just beneath the ear opening. No manner of finger-and-thumb dexterity could coax it out. I feared to contemplate the fate of my other ear.

Once in the locker room, I blurted, "I sliced my foot on the pool ladder!"

Another lifeguard, who was getting ready for her shift, ran over. She commanded, "Don't walk, I'll get you something."

I stared at a widening wound that threatened eruption.

The lifeguard rushed back and wrapped my enlarged, pounding foot.

No wonder kids beg their parents for Barbie-doctor scrubs.

I prayed my new friends would not come in and see me like this.

Before the staff could make too much of it, I wobbled outside. A path of water droplets followed me to my getaway car.

At home, I hurried and hopped around on my right foot while shaking my head hard to the left side, trying to knock out the wax piece while searching for the ear syringe. I wished my yogini (yoga teacher) could see me then—who says I don't have perfect balance?

But the more I tried to dislodge that persistent glob, the wilier that wax became.

Also, my ankle swelled. With both ears stuffed with wax, I could hear my heartbeat.

In desperation, I called my sister Molly. She didn't answer.

I texted her: "Please call back. Bring your sandals that divide the big toes. I cannot wear any of mine.... And, by the way, do you have an ear syringe?"

Molly rushed over, "Keep the sandals, they have had their day. But if you don't mind, I will take back my new turkey baster."

So, I avoided going to the emergency room using salt soak, a pair of vintage flip-flops, and an ear plunger—being careful not to extract my eardrum.

Molly's quick effort saved me a lot of time, money, and humiliation.

Tomorrow I would ask my sister why she brought over a turkey baster instead of an ear syringe.

Or maybe I wouldn't, since Molly was never one to play with dolls.

-Jill Morgan Clark

Really Young for That

I WAS 43 YEARS old. Subsequent doctors and nurses would look at my medical history and say, "That's really young for something like that to happen."

It all started one morning as I headed to work. I felt this odd feeling—not really a pain, but an unusual sensation under my armpit. I worked at a bookstore, so I went to the medical section and looked up my symptoms. The best match for my symptoms said the sensation should stop after 12 to 15 minutes. It had already been nagging me for about 3 hours, so I gave it 45 more minutes. I figured now that I knew how long it was supposed to last, it would follow the rules. It didn't. Finally, I sidled up to a manager and said in my low, calm, even way, "I don't want to alarm anyone, but I think I may be having a heart attack."

Soon, in an emergency room, they hooked me up to machines to monitor my heartbeat and lines for fluids; and made me take a nitroglycerin pill, which gave me a terrible migraine headache. EKG was fine. Bloodwork was fine. Everything looked fine. At the end of the day, the E.R. doctor said to me, "I really don't think your symptoms are heart-related, but if this were my brother and he went home now, I'd be really mad at him." Seed of doubt planted, I stayed the night for a stress test.

The next morning, I was on a treadmill. I had all these sticky sensors with wires stuck to my chest and abdomen and I'm sure I looked just like Lee Majors in the opening credits for the Six Million Dollar Man.

Except, the sensation under my arm became an actual pain.

"Okay, that's really hurting now," I said.

"Gives us another minute," they said.

"No, really, I mean it. It's starting to hurt pretty badly," I said.

"Another 30 seconds," they said.

When they finally let me off the treadmill, they tried to give me another nitroglycerin pill. I balked. "That gave me a headache that's much worse than the pain in my side," I said.

"The headache won't kill you," they said.

Fair enough.

Later that day, they said, "It looks like you might have a little blockage. We need to do a catheterization in the morning to get a better look."

In case you don't know, this sort of catheterization is a puncture wound in your groin, where they enter the large major artery that runs the length of the body. If they don't do it right, you can bleed out in a matter of seconds. No big deal.

The next morning, I laid on this table while they were snaking a camera up my torso from the inside. I watched it all on a monitor on the wall. It's like being your own science show. Yes, I was awake for all of it.

Then they shot this—ink? Something like ink into my heart so they could see where any blockage was. They warned me it would be warm. It was. It hit my heart, which dispersed this shock of warmth across my chest and arms, dissipating as it got farther away from my heart.

It was AWESOME! Whoosh! I've never done drugs and I don't even like the way alcohol makes me feel. But I'm telling you, if not for the dangerous puncture wound in my groin, I'd do this recreationally.

The medical people were at my feet during all this, snaking cameras and shooting ink up my torso through my groin. Eventually, a very serious doctor came up to my head and said, very seriously, "Mr. Orts, you have a completely blocked artery in your heart."

I said, "Huh. Who knew?"

The very serious doctor continued, "We're consulting with some other doctors to see if we think we can open it up with a balloon or if we have to do open heart surgery."

"The former, please," I said.

The doctor scowled, seriously, and said, "Of course," and he went to talk about me behind my back with the other doctors.

Long story short, they were able to open it up with a stent rather than sawing through my ribcage, cracking me wide open, and touching my exposed heart with their latexed hands. Within an hour, they were able to diagnose and solve the problem. Thankfully. They said that subtle nagging sensation under my armpit wasn't exactly a heart attack, but they also said to say it wasn't one was splitting hairs.

Afterward, the nurses and orderlies passed my chart around among themselves and said things like, "Oh wow."

"Who is this? This guy? Wow."

"That's amazing."

At the age of 43, I was amazing.

And new doctors and nurses, in subsequent years, look at my medical history and say, "That's really young for something like that to happen."

I answer, "Yeah. I've heard."

-Neil Ellis Orts

I Am Not An Athlete

I AM NOT AN athlete.

This isn't due to lack of effort. I've attempted almost everything involving a ball one can kick, pitch, or run after, and even some sports without a ball altogether. Softball saw me sweating in the outfield, while baseball had me catching with a glove two sizes too small jammed on my hand. Horseback riding left me dented after I got kicked in the leg, and basketball gave me a healthy fear of projectiles aimed anywhere near my head.

However, even with every sport I've tried, I still wouldn't say I'm athletic. My participation never matched my proficiency. Tennis resulted in me flashing any onlookers when my skirt flew up as I scrambled around with my racquet. Soccer mainly consisted of me panting in the dust as everyone else raced ahead. Volleyball reversed everything I had learned from basketball. I eagerly rushed towards all incoming projectiles . . . that inevitably smacked me in the face.

I've even given running a chance. Not on an actual team. I've yet to reach that level of insanity. But my enthusiasm for a sport that eliminated any potential concussions due to flying balls was quickly squashed by the sweaty, wheezing, uncomfortable nightmare of jogging. No one looks happy when they run. If someone actually enjoys racing from one arbitrary point to the other, I applaud them. They've managed to delude themselves into loving running far better than I ever could.

Thankfully, I eventually stumbled upon a sport that didn't require endless jogging. A sport that praised attempting over mastering. At the competitive level, Taekwondo, a style of martial arts, is a beautiful display of dedication in both physical and mental prowess.

At my level, Taekwondo provided an hour of physical activity every Tuesday and Thursday. I would have taken Wednesday classes too, but those went beyond the intermediate standard I was comfortably hovering in.

Not that I didn't try to push myself. I did and quickly regretted it. Even a week after an intense round of kicking plastic targets while pop music blared throughout the dojo, my ankle still twinged painfully. My attempts to stoically walk it off, while also complaining loudly so everyone knew how brave I was, failed when the ache refused to disappear. A few days after that ill-fated class, landing on my foot awkwardly led to some choice words in front of a scandalized gym teacher. He would have clutched his pearls if public school teachers made anywhere near enough to afford such luxuries.

After acknowledging the pain was so distressing it had me swearing like a sailor, I found myself in the doctor's office. The clinical scent of sanitizer overwhelmed me, and my medical gown crinkled every time I moved. While waiting on the X-ray results, I kicked my legs out from the medical table I was perched on. Without any weight on it, my ankle felt fine, and I appreciated the momentary release as my legs swung in and out.

Flex in.

Flex out.

Flex in.

Flex out.

Flex—

Bang!

Startled, I paused mid-kick as the doctor returned from examining my X-rays. Hopefully, with a favorable diagnosis too. I'd already missed a Taekwondo class for this appointment. Ignoring my still-raised legs - I doubt I was the oddest patient she'd walked in on that day - she squirted out some hand sanitizer and turned to face me with a smile.

"Well," she said, "I just finished looking over your X-rays, and I have some good news!"

"Mhmm," I muttered, trying to remember if I needed to wash my Taekwondo uniform before the next class. While I remained at the intermediate level, I still made sure to sweat. For better or for worse, the smelly proof was evident by each workout's end.

"We can get you into surgery in as soon as three months!"

"What?" I stammered. No longer thinking of laundry, I was instead plagued by several questions.

Did a medical license corrupt one's perception of 'good news?'

How was three months 'soon?'

And why did I need surgery for a minor ankle twinge?

"Well," the doctor said, tucking a loose curl behind her ear. "Think of your bones like a candy bar." I nodded, appreciating her metaphor. Evidently, this doctor understood her audience. "If you keep pummeling the candy bar, it will eventually crumble. Although everything might seem okay because the wrapper keeps the candy bar intact, if you peel that back, everything spills out."

I stared, still confused, and now craving chocolate.

"The candy bars are your bones," the doctor finally explained. "Your ankle bone, to be precise. Most likely from something continually hitting your foot, the bone has weakened beneath the cartilage. To fix the affected area, you'll need surgery."

Briefly, I thought back to my biweekly engagement with a punching bag. Recently, I'd started favoring repetitively attacking it, with my foot slamming into the firm material again and again.

Zoning back in, I realized the doctor was still talking. Suddenly picking up on her last few words, I asked her to repeat herself.

"Oh, you'll need to avoid high-impact activities," the doctor reiterated. Before she could continue, I nervously interrupted her.

"Could you define 'high impact?'"

Tapping a finger to her lips, the doctor considered my question. "Anything that could cause significant exertion. For example, strenuous activity, including, but not limited to, sudden jumping and jolting movements that expend pressure on your joints."

"And for how long should I avoid these activities?" I thought of Taekwondo, and how essential sudden jumping and jolting motions were to participate in even beginner-level exercises.

"Forever," the doctor stated.

"For... ever?" I repeated.

"Forever," she confirmed.

After staring at each other for a moment, she moved to break the awkward silence. "Oh, this doesn't mean an end to exercising, though!"

"Really?" I asked, temporarily relieved.

"A lot of patients enjoy jogging!" she exclaimed with a smile.

If I gagged at the thought of running, that's between me and the doctor who threw me a concerned glance.

-Teagan Durkin

Beach Day Blunders

S TATISTICALLY, EVERY VACATION SHOULD be horrible.

Simply examine the factors. The stress that goes into planning any vacation, however small or large, paired with the impossible expectations of creating lasting memories within a few short days, should inevitably spell disaster. This is without even examining the general catastrophes of any getaway: someone gets sunburned at the beach, wanders off while hiking a scenic trail, or is willingly scammed into buying a souvenir that will shatter in their suitcase.

However, through some miraculous improbability, I have enjoyed rather pleasant vacations. Sparing the odd hiccup or two—forgetting to pack enough underwear, or frantically pulling the car over so I can upchuck on the side of the road—my trips have been relaxing escapes with no grievous injuries to myself or others.

Except for one vacation.

It was a sunny day at the beach. Not boiling enough that the sand burned my toes, but hot enough to enjoy the cool tide lapping around my ankles. Sighing, I turned my head away from the ocean to glance back at my dad and little sister further up in the dunes. The umbrella's circus tent colors of red and yellow made them easy enough to spot against the otherwise beige landscape. My brother and I, old and smart enough to make good decisions but young and dumb enough to not follow them, had been left alone in the surf.

The first mistake of the day.

"Hey, look at this!" my brother called out.

"Sure," I replied. Pausing in my search for small crabs to put down people's swimsuits, I proceeded to give him my full attention.

The second mistake of the day.

Holding out his hands, he showed me a thin piece of wood, roughly the size of a squished watermelon. It appeared he had found a piece of driftwood, given how battered and flimsy it looked, but he then explained it was a skimboard.

Intrigued, I asked, "How does it work?"

The third mistake of the day . . . . At this point, I should stop counting.

"Watch," he smirked. Running along the shallow waves, he suddenly threw the skimboard down. Jumping onto it, he skidded across the water before nimbly hopping off. His peacocking complete, he held the skimboard out and encouraged me to try riding it.

"Okay," I conceded, placing the board down and stepping a few paces away. Remembering what my brother had done, I raced forward across the sand and prepared for a smooth, almost floating, slide across the small swells. My toes touching the skimboard's edge, I could almost envision that graceful glide—then promptly tripped and rolled my ankle.

"Cheese and crackers!" I screamed just as a wave swept over me. Sitting up, I started sputtering out briny water and seaweed. Raising my ankle, I winced as I noticed an angry red line. Trying to flex it, I immediately uttered more charcuterie-centric swear words as a splintering pain throbbed through my foot.

A rolled ankle is not the worst injury in the world. Or, it wouldn't have been if I hadn't rolled the ankle I had surgery on the past year.

And, after months of physical therapy, my doctor just recently cleared me to walk on without a boot.

Just in time for this beach trip.

"Maybe it just looks bad?" my brother offered. Intelligently, he was out of arm's reach from where I was still sprawled in the waves.

"Maybe," I said optimistically, ignoring the twinging ache that gripped my foot whenever I experimentally moved my ankle. I would remain optimistic until someone told me otherwise. Unfortunately, that time came far too soon.

After limping back to the house, my dad fished a medical boot out of the closet and slapped it on my ankle. At that point, as I could only limp across the sand and stare longingly at the ocean, I amused myself by seeing how long I could glare at my brother without blinking.

I managed to reach a minute. Spite is a powerful motivator.

-Teagan Durkin

Three Small Holes

I ENTERED THE HOSPITAL for what I had thought would be a simple arthroscopic knee surgery. Was told I could drive myself home and within three weeks I'd be wind sailing, which sounded miraculous since I could never right myself on a board. Instead, I woke up and discovered they cut my entire left leg in half and hoisted over my body by some ratchet gadget, which left me in a moment of shock.

I called the nurse and asked what happened—there were supposed to be three small holes in my knees, not this sliced leg—she said I'd have to ask the surgeon the next day. I asked her to hand me my medical chart, which she did with great reluctance, and I realized something terrible happened and I ended up with major ACL surgery.

The next morning, the surgeon was apologetic. He had no idea my knee was so bad and assured me that he gave me plastic surgery like he did his wife, and I'd hardly see a scar. A scar was the least of my worries. I wanted to know when I'd be released! One week. But I wouldn't be able to return to my special education teaching job for a year... nor windsurf, nor drive, nor attend the writer's workshop, nor the big biking and hiking trip I was all geared up for; my truck packed and ready to go when I left this hospital with *three tiny holes* in my knee.

The next day, one nurse tried to cheer me up by saying I looked like Jacqueline Kennedy. The other nurse insisted there was no resemblance, and I squeezed my morphine button, hoping to slip away to a better place.

During the evening, I woke to my new roommate, an unpleasant elderly woman with zero interest in exchanging pleasantries. Instead, she seemed to believe I was her worthless daughter, Delores, and yelled obscenities at me for being such a lazy daughter, a good-for-nothing thief, and a rotten liar. I tried assuring her I was not Delores but she picked up her plastic water bottle, threw it at my leg—which she could not miss—and yelled, "There you go with your lies, Delores." I howled in pain. She laughed with delight.

Throughout the night, she emptied everything on her tray. Her water glass burst on my leg which remained uncast, just swollen and stapled. She even threw her false teeth at me. I rang for the nurse, and she walked right past me to the old woman and asked if I had been bothering her. "She's worthless. Always has been. That lazy Delores!"

Finally, the nurse, who was already peeved that her colleague thought I looked like Jacqueline Kennedy, walked over, and told me I shouldn't upset her so much. She replaced everything on her tray and during the night, all of it ended up once again smashing into my leg. There was no way she could miss.

The next morning when the surgeon visited, her water bottle and teeth were still on my bed, and I explained what had happened. He was furious and screamed for a nurse. "This is a fifty-thousand-dollar surgery. Get her out of here. She needs a room by herself!" He then told the nurse to increase my pain medication, and I slipped away into another morphine-laced world.

In the middle of the night, a strange man entered my room and told me it was time to get up and walk to the bathroom. I hadn't been out of bed, had no cast, and had zero interest in trying to walk to the bathroom. He became quite angry. "It's the only way you'll learn to walk. Get out of bed!"

When I didn't budge, he hauled me out of bed, and I screamed so loud several people came running to see what was going on. Security officers led the man away. Someone gave me an injection. A woman came and told me to sign papers. She apologized that this man had escaped from the psychiatric ward. I knew I didn't want to sign the papers, but she took my hand, put the pen between my fingers, and mumbled, "I'll help you get your signature on the correct lines." For a moment I missed the old woman, and then slipped off into another drug-induced sleep, hoping it'd free me of this infernal reality.

-Diane Payne

If You're Happy

WHEN I FOUND OUT that my nonverbal autistic son also had asthma, I was mad. In fact, I think the first words that came out of my mouth were "This is so stupid!" I didn't understand why someone who already had challenges communicating with us would also have challenges with breathing. It didn't make any sense and I spent a lot of time being bitter about it.

One day, my son had a severe asthma attack. We rushed him to the Emergency Room. By now, they knew us pretty well, as we struggled to get his asthma under control. I spent a lot of time explaining to my son what would happen next and talking him through all the pokes, prods, and strangers that would enter the room.

The respiratory therapist came in to do a breathing treatment. My five-year-old son looked up at him and started singing, "If you're happy and you know it...." He paused and looked up at the guy, who couldn't make out the words my son was trying to sing. My son screamed and pushed the air mask away.

"What's going on?" he asked.

"Umm... I think he wants you to sing?" I replied.

"Sing?"

"Yes. He wants you to sing 'If You're Happy and You Know It'," I said calmly. As if this was a very normal request for your respiratory therapist. He tried to put the mask back on and my son again screamed and pushed it away. "I think we have to sing!"

I belted out the words. My son turned to me and smiled. I understood him! He began singing and clapping along. The respiratory therapist soon joined in. I finished with a very dramatic slowed down "If you're happy and you know it...then you really ought to show it!!!" My son giggled behind the oxygen mask.

When we finished all the verses, he clapped and said "Again!" The respiratory therapist looked at me to interpret.

"He wants us to sing again!" so we kept going. Soon, a nurse came in and joined us. It became a whole production and anyone who walked by heard us singing. My son refused to let us stop until his breathing treatment was complete, so we sang again and again.

How often was this song sung in the ER? Probably not much. Had a child having one of the worst days of his life ever sung it? At least once! My son was in the hospital. He couldn't breathe, his vitals plummeted, and he struggled to communicate with those around him. Despite all these challenges, he was happy, and he wanted everyone to know it!

-Heather G Preece

Hip Replacement

My clothes somewhere far away in a plastic bag.
I lie beneath blue wrap in the intense light of the OR,
my feet fastened into adjustable stirrups.
No feeling in my legs or feet.
I try moving them.
Nothing.

Immediately I decided NOT to try that again.
Actually, what difference does it make?
This will be over soon, or will I stay paralyzed forever?
Drops of water slide across my temples into my ears.
Brief whirring, then the smell of bone dust.
Gone is something inside me for 74 years.
I close my eyes, breathe deeply, let go of all I can think of.
Then my nose itches.
I pull at my mask and scratch, hoping no one notices.

Blue wrap rustles. Tapping, then banging.
Is this really happening to me while others have lunch?
Voices—numbers (leg length?).
More numbers (score of the Sharks game last night?).
Social on Friday. Tina's last day.

Surgeon's voice now absent.
He must be off fist-bumping the next patient.
Eight knees and two hips, all in a day's work,
Tuesdays, Thursdays and alternate Fridays.

Anesthesiologist at my head says, *They're closing you up now.*
Tell them to make it nice and neat to heal quickly, I say
between yawns I cannot control.

Sewing up takes as long as all the rest together.
Several pairs of practiced arms roll me onto a bed
that begins moving toward recovery
like a boat on some irregular course.

-Marianne Brems

Pre-Op

I STORMED OUT OF my husband's pre-op room. Though tempted, I did not slam the door. I walked up to the nurses' station. "Can you just poison him? Put him out of my misery? Or can I strangle him?"

The startled looks from the nurses told me they weren't used to wives threatening to kill husbands, and they weren't sure if I was kidding. I wasn't even sure I was kidding.

I had to get out of there. "How much trouble is it if I go out this main door?"

"If you go out, someone has to come and bring you back in."

I couldn't even run away. I stood there, shaking.

My excuse? I'd been up for over 24 hours, and in that time, I'd had to deal with dread, agitation, and anxiety—my husband's, our children's, and my own. I could feel my fingernails sliding down the chalkboard of my life. Anger bubbled and boiled, heavy and viscous, like a mud pot in Yellowstone. I knew the anger was really fear, but it was so much easier to be angry.

His excuse—he had a brain tumor. So yeah, his excuse eclipsed mine.

Only six days before, we met with his doctor at the Veterans' Administration Clinic in Casper, WY. It was a regularly scheduled appointment, that given weather conditions, we might have canceled. But I had seen changes in my husband's behavior that were atypical and both of us were frightened.

"We'll do a lot more testing, but today we just have time for an MRI. That will help us know what is going on."

Asked if I'd like to observe, I declined, longing for a few minutes' respite.

The doctor ran past me to the MRI building. My stomach clenched. This can't be good.

Returning more slowly, the Doctor beckoned me into a conference room next door.

"Your husband has a tumor covering the entire right hemisphere of his brain. When he comes out, I'll show you both."

We stared at the screen on the computer. Half his brain was white.

Surgery was scheduled for Monday, three days away. Our daughters arrived on the weekend. Kristi, at age 47, the calmer of the two, drove them up from Denver.

Debbie, our eldest, 50 and a bit of a drama queen, struggled. Her partner of five years died the year before from stomach cancer. Now her father, the man she most loved and admired, was sick.

Sunday evening, we traveled the 50 miles to Casper. I sent the kids out for hamburgers to eat in our motel room. After supper, the kids went to their rooms. We watched some TV.

At midnight, my husband told me it was time to go to the hospital.

"No, your surgery isn't until 9 a.m. We have plenty of time."

At 1 a.m., he said, "We need to go now."

"No, your surgery isn't until 9 a.m."

"If you won't take me, I'll just go myself."

I got up, got dressed, and walked him out to the car.

"Oh, I thought it was just downstairs."

"No. We have to drive to the hospital."

We arrived at the hospital at 2 a.m. It was closed, so we found our way down to the Emergency Entrance waiting room.

My husband paced back and forth, checking doors, juggling handles, trying to get in. "Maybe this one is open."

"No, Honey. They aren't open now."

"We should go down the hall and check."

"No. It's too early."

"You aren't the one having brain surgery. You could at least check and see."

Four a.m., five hours before we are even supposed to be there. Almost in tears, I asked if the Emergency Room could admit him. They agreed.

Because he was scheduled for surgery, there wasn't any medication they could give him to calm him, I was tired, but my heart ached.

"Don't they have cups in here? I'm thirsty."

"You can't have anything to eat or drink now. Not after midnight."

"But I'm thirsty!"

So was I, but I needed to keep him safe for the surgery. I became both his protector and his adversary.

My husband had taken to reading Bob Dylan's lyrics, because, in his words, "if he won a Nobel Prize, Dylan must be worth reading". I looked up songs by Dylan on my iPad and read the lyrics to him. The last real discussion of his life was about what those lyrics meant.

But it's hard to kill time reading aloud, and he was once again conscious of the loss of control over his life.

I stepped outside the room and asked a nurse for a glass of water for me. She brought me a glass of ice water and I drank deep, the cold water easing my parched throat. Guilt washed over me. I couldn't return to the room with water, so I tossed the rest.

The hospital personnel were really great to us. Even though he wasn't scheduled to be at the hospital until 9 a.m., someone from radiology showed up at 7 a.m. to take him for his first MRI of the day. I sent a text to our daughters to tell them we were already at the hospital.

I suspect Debbie drank a six-pack, or two, the night before. She walked up to the hospital later. Kristi came quickly.

Nurses took my husband to the pre-op room. It was still early. Kristi and I sat on the edge of the chairs in the waiting area. I allowed myself the luxury of a cup of coffee.

A pre-op nurse hurried out. "Has your husband had anything to eat or drink since midnight?"

"No. Though he's been begging for a glass of water."

"Okay, when we asked him if he'd had anything to eat, he said he'd had a hamburger and fries for breakfast."

"No, that was supper last night around 6:30 p.m. He hasn't eaten or had anything to drink since then."

"Oh, good." Relief showed on her face. "You can come back in a few minutes."

When I walked into the pre-op room, he saw a container of liquid in my hand. I poured my coffee down the drain and, not seeing a waste basket, set the paper cup on the counter by the sink.

He looked at Kristi. "See that cup on the counter? Pick it up and fill it with water and bring it here."

She looked over at me, and I nodded. I was so tired of fighting. So, she gave him a drink of water. He made a show of drinking the entire glass.

Looking at me, he said, "See how easy that was? It's a control thing, just like in the Air Force."

I was DONE!

Later, Kristi told me she and her dad could hear me outside, threatening to kill him.

"I started asking him about the Air Force and his time in the service."

I smiled. I had raised a smart daughter.

-Vickie Goodwin

THAT ADVENTURE TOOK AN UNEXPECTED TURN...

If you think it's the journey and not the destination, maybe you've never flown on commercial airlines.

That's Fine

A T 6 MONTHS PREGNANT, there wasn't much I could do on a cruise ship – I knew that going in. Fancy drinks weren't an option. The water slides were out. At the very least, I could enjoy a relaxing maternity massage and see a comedy show or two. But I wasn't boarding the ship for myself. This trip was for the family. Mandatory family fun, as we all jokingly called it.

Specifically, we were vacationing with my maternal side of the family. This included my grandad, a man carrying a portable oxygen tank who often bickered with my grandma who had dementia. My mom tried to act as a peacemaker and reign the two of them in. I think she was losing her sanity in the process though. I was sure she would develop a nervous tic along with her throbbing forehead vein by the time we finished the cruise.

My husband, alongside my mother, was the only able-bodied person to push the wheelchairs and drag the heavy luggage, which was a slow, painstaking process as we boarded the ship and made our way through the long corridor to our cabins on embarkment day. Given my condition, they assigned me to push the stroller and soothe our toddler.

Our first day at sea was the craziest. starting when my toddler threw a fit, yelling "I WANT TO GO HOME!" I figured I'd settle her by grabbing some breakfast from the upstairs buffet. My husband offered to stay with her while I went to grab a bite of food and bring it back to our room where she could continue to unleash her wrath on her parents instead of the unsuspecting vacationers – at least until she calmed down. That was the plan but, of course, plans aren't always set in stone.

I fought through the crowded cafeteria and picked out her favorites – strawberries, cantaloupes, bananas, the works. On my return to our room with a fruit bowl in hand, housekeeping had replaced my dear hubby and daughter. *What?* Where had they gone? We were in the middle of the Atlantic Ocean with no Wi-Fi. Communication was a nightmare, sometimes impossible. I tried knocking on my grandparents' door, but no answer. My mom's room was also unoccupied. I traversed the entire ship, all levels, on a wild goose chase to locate any of my missing family members. At some point, I took a break, stopping in front of the ship's spa. I inquired if they had maternity massage services. A lady at the counter scanned me up and down.

"No," she said. "You're too far along. Can't risk inducing you into labor."

"But I'm only six months..."

I think she thought I lied because she raised her eyebrows like she was unconvinced. "Nope. Sorry, ma'am. We can't do it."

I was disappointed but I wasn't a confrontational person by nature, so I simply shrugged and walked away. At least I could still attend the comedy show...

I spent the entire first half of the day on elevators, scaling up and down, a lone pregnant woman still trying to find my family, receiving a lot of apprehensive looks on the elevators, eyes widened as they leveled on my stomach. Their thoughts were palpable: "She's a ticking time bomb!"

My suspicions were confirmed by one woman who commented, "You're brave for being here. I'd be worried about delivering the baby on the ship."

Gee, thanks...

"I'm only six months."

"Oh. Huh. Well, still..."

An awkward silence ensued.

After a while, I couldn't just hold the fruit bowl anymore. I ended up eating the contents. I was pregnant... after all. Couldn't resist food when it was right in front of me. It was almost lunchtime now anyway.

By noon, I had a detailed map of the ship etched in my brain, all ten floors charted. The soles of my feet ached from walking too long in flip-flops. The cleaning staff long finished and I needed a rest, so I inserted my key card to open the door to my room. When I walked in, I finally found them, my husband and daughter.

"Oh, my goodness! Where were you guys? I searched for you all over the ship!"

"We were at the casino," my husband explained. Our daughter played with her toys sprawled across the floor. I figured the room wouldn't stay tidy for long – a reality of parenthood that I was used to. At least she seemed happier now. I took a seat on our bed, finally lifting my abused feet off the floor. Sweet relief.

"Why the casino?"

"Because your grandad left his oxygen tank to hold his spot at a slot machine and couldn't remember where it was."

What?!

"Well, did he get it back? That's kind of important."

"I don't know. Your mom and I got separated while we were looking for it."

"Oh, goodness... He's always losing that thing."

"I know!"

"What are we going to do?" I asked. "Should I go look too?"

"No, we will get separated again. Plus, what if they already found it?"

Good point. I knew I wasn't ready to do more walking, my feet swelled. Still, I wished we could know for sure.

In a way, it was ironic that my grandad left his oxygen in a casino since he was, in essence, gambling his life. *How could he be so careless? That device is his lifeline. Doesn't he realize that?*

"And guess what he said?" my husband added.

"What?"

"He said 'Oh, it's fine. It's not like anyone's going to steal it. It's not that valuable.'"

"It's valuable to *him*," I mentioned.

"Yeah, that's exactly what I told him!"

There was a knock at the door. Knowing that pulling myself off the bed would take too long, my husband jumped to answer it. My mom stood in the doorway.

"Hey, what happened? Did he get his oxygen back?" he asked her.

"Huh? Oh, Yeah, we found that ages ago. He's fine. But now grandma lost her key card again."

"What? Where?"

"At the casino."

Again, with the casino.

"Wait a minute... what do you mean she lost it '*again*'?" I chimed in. I hated being out of the loop, not knowing what happened all day.

"She already lost it 3 times today," mom explained. "The staff at guest services know us very well."

I pinched the bridge of my nose and sighed.

"Alright, let's drop off little one at the onboard daycare and go look for it," I suggested. My husband shook his head. "What?"

"I already tried to drop her off when I was looking for the oxygen tank. She wasn't having it."

Weird. She loved attending preschool back home.

"What do you mean? She's supposed to go there so we can see the comedy show later," I said.

"Well, that's not happening." He shrugged.

"I can't babysit," my mom added. "I'm adult-sitting my elderly parents, which is proving much harder than I thought it would be."

"Okay, so no comedy shows then." I didn't want to go without hubby. No massage either. My lower eyelid twitched, my voice raising an octave when I said, "That's fine."

-S.J. Walker

Hold the Salt

I WATCHED MY TOES bobbing on the glittering surface of the Dead Sea, held afloat by minerals and saline so densely concentrated that nothing but bacteria survive in its depths. Eventually, I made my way to the beach.

Barefoot, dressed in cutoffs and string bikini top, I headed to the parking lot. No sign of my group's bus, a dilapidated tin can of a vehicle, anywhere. I had no clothes, no shoes, no money, no passport, and, as it was 1977, no cell phone. What I did have was...salt.

Crusty, abrasive salt in every crevice of my body, rubbing my sunburned thighs raw with every step. I couldn't remember the name of our hostel because it was in Hebrew. All I knew was that it was somewhere in the Negev Desert.

Eventually, a fellow American took pity and contacted the authorities in Jerusalem, who tracked down my tour group. The bus had to come back for me. The tour leaders learned to count teenagers before disembarking, and I learned that there was such a thing as beach showers at the Dead Sea. I didn't notice them because... my glasses were on the bus.

-Jennifer Shneiderman

One (Un)lucky Day in Kuala Lumpur

A T THE END OF June 2023, I went to Kuala Lumpur with 2 friends. We took different flights from different cities. I packed everything I needed but MYR cash; the currency used in Malaysia. My friend would help me exchange money for MYR since there was no money changer in my city. I wasn't worried. After having visited Malaysia in 2022, this would be easy. I packed 2 phones with e-wallets, MYR 31 from my previous trip, an amount of Indonesian currency, and ATM cards in my bag.

I landed around 9 a.m. My friends' flights would land after 12 a.m. Immigration checking had a long line. It took more than an hour for me to clear. In my calculation, MYR 31 would be enough to get me a simple meal, a train ticket to Putra Jaya, and then another train ticket to KL Sentral. The train tickets would cost MYR 23, so a meal could be MYR 7-8. I also had e-wallets. According to Indonesian news, I could use both or one of them here.

As I scanned the food arcade, everything looked mouthwatering. I looked around the arcade twice and chose curry rice. The aroma really enticed me. I checked the menu list, it's MYR 5, plus 2.5 with rice. The kitchen staff asked me if I wanted additional dishes and I said yes. My own stupid decision and the start of my misery. The bill said 12 MYR.

Well, now I didn't have enough cash to buy a train ticket, but I was not worried at all. I had e-wallets.

I went to the KLIA Express booth to buy a ticket to the Putra Jaya station. I asked if I could pay using my e-wallets. The staff checked, and they did not have them listed on their cashless payment system. So, I bought a ticket to Putra Jaya and browsed for cheaper options to transfer to KL Sentral with my leftover MYR. I found a cheap one. Someone told me I had to stop at Chan Sow

Lin station to get the next train to KL Sentral. I was sleepy, so I slept during the trip while leaning on my bag.

Then I transferred to another train. From here, I started to get disoriented. I asked the officer, but I thought she gave me the wrong directions. I asked someone else, another passenger, and she said I should get on the train she was in, the train I just got off. It meant I needed to go back to where I was. Okay. I got on the train. The girl told me which stop I needed to get off, and then which train I should transfer.

The train stopped at Hang Tuah Station. I got off and realized that I didn't have my bag with me. I panicked. That bag had my passport, money, ATM card, and return flight ticket. I only had my luggage with my clothes and shoes, plus MYR 3 in my pocket.

The station staff took me to the complaint center. The man at the complaint center received my report. He asked me to write my phone number so that he could contact me later, in case the bag was found. He then checked if my phone was active by calling the number I just gave him. It failed. I tried to check his number, but it failed as well. He told me he wouldn't be able to contact me later if my phone number couldn't be contacted. I guessed there was something wrong or a misunderstanding. My heart sank to the floor. My mind totally blank. Sitting down in front of the complaint center, I broke into tears. Not knowing if it would help bring my bag back, but needing to share the load on my mind, I contacted my friends I would be meeting and a couple of local people I knew. I just needed to share this to help lift the weight in my mind.

It was a dark hour in my life. In a foreign country, no money, and no family members. I cried hopelessly, waiting for a miracle to come, but preparing for the worst.

Then, a local friend told me she sent her friend to pick me up. Oh my goodness gracious! I would ask him to take me to the police station to file a report. I needed an emergency letter to get around without my passport. Then I was told that they found my bag at the Chan Sow Lin station! I was so elated! I just got a second chance to live.

Long story short, my new friend drove me to Chan Sow Lin. We talked on the way, and I found out he was actually Indonesian but lived in Malaysia. He was so funny that I forgot a bit about my misery. He asked if I cried, and I nodded "of course!" Then we laughed.

I got back my bag. He left, and then my travel mates picked me up at the station to go to the hotel. What luck to start my vacation!

-Jamaatun Rohmah

Assumptions

W HILE VACATIONING IN INDIA, our rental car company sent us a car. As is customary in India, a driver came with it as well. Bharati, the driver, was a peculiar man.

Bharati was always punctual and arrived at our guesthouse when we needed him. But he had a horrendous sense of the city. When we wanted to go to a well-known music store, he asked pedestrians for directions before setting off.

On the way, he would frequently hop out of the car to ask passers-by for the correct route. After numerous stops, he managed to get us to our destination. Bharati spoke only in Tamil, the language of the state. Since my husband was fluent in Tamil and I could only understand it, I left the communications up to him.

When we wanted to visit cousins who lived in the heart of the city, Bharati again stumbled for directions. We made several stops for clarification. At a traffic light, he rolled down the window, leaned out, and asked the auto-rickshaw driver for directions.

When I wanted to go to the most popular clothing store in the city, he floundered yet again.

I could take it no longer. I spoke to my husband in another Indian language, Kannada. "A barely fifteen-minute drive is taking over half an hour," I said as he drove us through town.

"What kind of driver is he?" I ranted to my husband about Bharati's incompetence.

"He doesn't know a thing! He is useless. He shouldn't be a driver." I went on and on.

A few days later, we drove six hours away to Bangalore, where the local language is Kannada. Once in Bangalore, Bharati needed directions to my father-in-law's home, so once again, he rolled down his window.

In Tamil, Bharati asked an adjacent driver for directions. The Bangalorean driver spat out directions in rapid Kannada. Bharati nodded, thanked him, and drove on.

My throat went dry while I sat in shocked silence.

-Viji K. Chary

Marshmallow Races

C AMPING IS SUPPOSED TO be fun. Nature lovers adore sleeping under the stars in the wilderness. Outfitters' advertisements promise cozy evenings by an open fire. However, my first such excursion veered off script within thirty minutes of unpacking the tent.

As one who prefers reading by electric lights to swatting bugs in the dark, I have never been tempted to join the ranks of camping enthusiasts. By my senior year in high school, I had filled every inch of my bedroom shelves with novels and poetry. In contrast, my three younger siblings stuffed their closets with pup tents, camp stoves, lanterns, fishing poles, collapsible bowls, utility knives, canteens, and sleeping bags.

After field testing their gear in the backyard on numerous occasions, my brother and sisters clamored for a "real camping expedition." The proposed destination was Staunton River State Park, only 18 miles away. The facility was rather primitive, but proximity trumped scant amenities.

Since Dad worked until 5:30 PM on Saturdays, the threesome needed to recruit someone else to serve as a driver. Mom expressed a strong preference for spending summer days in a dwelling with air conditioning, a refrigerator, and running water. As the eldest and the only kid with a driver's license, I was the next target of their campaign. Weeks of pleading eventually wore me down. I agreed to serve as chauffeur one humid Saturday in June. We planned to set up camp and spend the day on our own. Dad would join us there after he got off work.

On arrival, our first challenge was finding level ground. Given the slope of our assigned campsite, we pitched the tents in a broad ravine. Hammering the tent stakes caused minor damage to several thumbs, but no one required supplies from the new deluxe first aid kit with bandages in six sizes.

Having established our base, the next order of business was a trek to the river, fishing poles in hand. Although I'm not emotionally attached to earthworms, I can't bring myself to bait a hook. Consequently, I served as a spectator, referee, and pack mule.

A ten-minute hike brought us to an undisturbed section of the waterway where brambles and weeds concealed red mud. The sucking sound under our feet came too late to save our tennis shoes. Spattered with muck, we hunted for dry rocks and positioned ourselves on the bank.

My brother Doug boasted he would catch dinner, although he had never gutted, boned, or scaled a fish. I snickered and rolled my eyes. In competitive families, such a response is equivalent to throwing down the gauntlet. As the youngest child and the only boy, Doug responded to challenges with reckless abandon. His enthusiastic first cast went wild—he hooked his thumb. Unfortunately, we neglected to bring the deluxe first aid kit with bandages in six sizes. I chose not to mention that he would need a tetanus shot on our return home.

While Doug and I wrestled with the wayward hook, my sister Dana redoubled her efforts to land the first catch of the day. After several unorthodox casting moves, she caught something and launched into a jig. We shouted encouragement and suggestions, which she disregarded. Yanking her pole, she whipped the line back into the shallows. A six-inch catfish thrashed in the muddy water. When she reached down to grapple with the captive, his fins stung her hand. An exuberant whoop morphed into a scream. Of course, that fish got away.

My sister Marie focused on a nibble from a so-called trophy bass when thunder rumbled in the distance. A glance at the storm clouds on the horizon convinced us to cut our riverside party short. As we trudged back, sporadic raindrops became a downpour, and we accelerated to a dead run.

Soaked by the time we reached the campsite, we dove into the nylon tents, which offered minimal protection. Water dripped from the canopy onto my nose with the steady rhythm of a metronome. On shifting positions, Marie and I discovered a large puddle in the center of our groundsheet. Within seconds, a river flowed under our sleeping bags. Yelps erupted from the adjacent pup tents as Dana and Doug found themselves at sea as well.

By mutual agreement, we piled into the car to wait out the storm. The sun emerged an hour later, and we followed suit. Shivering in bedraggled attire, we surveyed the picnic table loaded with remnants of our planned feast. The hot dogs, still hermetically sealed in plastic, were unscathed. However, every scrap of firewood was drenched. The buns were a soggy mass. Two cans of baked beans were undamaged, but the can opener had fallen into the muck and disappeared. The cling wrap on the bowl of potato salad had given way, submerging the contents. Someone had broken into the bag of marshmallows, so those were damp as well. The Hershey bars oozed through their paper wrappers, and the graham crackers resembled wet sand. S'mores were no longer on the menu.

We perched on the picnic table and glowered at the creek that flooded our tents. Doug vented his frustration by pitching a few marshmallows into the water. When they bobbed and drifted away, Marie suggested we race the rest. This proved somewhat problematic because all our "boats" were identical. After a few chaotic matches, we abandoned the competition.

Shortly thereafter, a raccoon ambled by on the opposite bank of the temporary stream. Lobbing the marshmallows to him proved more entertaining than racing. When our snack supply was exhausted, he trundled off, leaving us to the mosquitoes. Insect repellant never appeared in the ads for camping essentials.

Huddled on the rough boards of the table, we tried not to wiggle because the deluxe first aid kit with bandages in six sizes had no tweezers for splinter removal. When Dad arrived at dusk, the vote to abort was unanimous. Grumpy, damp, and exhausted, we broke camp and headed back to civilization.

After drying our gear in the sun for a few days, we repacked everything and stashed it in the garage. The sleeping bag I purchased for our doomed outing migrated to the back of my bedroom closet. Most of the other camping equipment gathered dust until it succumbed to mildew, rust, or obsolescence.

Several years ago, I came across my old sleeping bag when my husband and I were collecting items for a garage sale. A beaming teenager with purple cat-eye glasses pounced on that relic from my past. When I accepted her money and thanked her, my voice quavered. Allergies, no doubt.

-Elizabeth Spencer Spragins

Winter Wonderland

W HEN DICK AND CAROLYN invited Linda and me to join their family for winter cabin camping on Presidents' Day weekend, it sounded like fun. We did not know the family very well, but had been attending the same church for several years. Their youngest, Rick, was about six, close to our oldest, Tammy. Dick and Carolyn had two older girls, Dana and Beth. We had one younger boy, Doug, and a small spaniel mix, Sukie.

Dick and Carolyn were members of the Appalachian Trail Club, which gave them the privilege to rent any of the cabins that the Club owned near the Trail. The one they picked for this trip was a two-story cabin with parking only a few car lengths away. We wouldn't need backpacks; supplies could be carried directly from the cars across a small footbridge and up to the cabin door.

While the adults were getting everything into the cabin, Tammy needed to use the outhouse. Rick locked her in. When he finally let her out, she shoved him into the creek.

Although Rick had been the one soaked in freezing water, Tammy was the one feeling sick later that day. By evening, Linda was not feeling great, either. Linda's stomach felt uneasy enough that she spread newspapers on the floor beside her bed—just in case. All the beds were on the undivided second floor of this cabin.

Later that night, Linda needed those newspapers. In the dark, she couldn't see that Sukie considered them the most comfortable place to sleep. Carolyn screamed when a panicked, vomit-covered dog jumped onto her sleeping bag. Both husbands woke instantly. Confusion reigned.

Once we understood what happened, we helped Linda and Tammy down to the first floor and restarted the fires in the cookstove and fireplace. Dick and I spent hours the previous day sawing and splitting firewood, but we had not stocked enough to last the rest of the night. We two guys, in pajamas, boots, and gloves, replenished the inside wood pile while Carolyn cleaned up the vomit.

There are two possible consequences of an introduction like that. Yes, we are friends for life! (And the dozen or so subsequent trips all were vomit-free adventures of different types.)

-Chuck Gaston

Overseas Travel, the Down and Dirty

I F YOU CAN'T ABIDE discomfort, delays, and dystopian flights, stay home. If you can't stomach being restrained for eight hours by a seat belt, not being able to dislodge easily from your middle seat to potty or sharing your seat with the overly large buttocks of a stranger, then remain an armchair traveler. If you intensely dislike listening to snarly passengers argue over the upgrade they didn't receive, whiny babies who occasionally pierce the sound barrier, and inedible food served without a simultaneous drink to wash it down, don't board a plane taking you to an international site to board a cruise ship.

Yet, if you long to see Sicilian splendors, to scoot in a boat over rippled blue water in Gozo's caves, or to scoop chocolate from a tartufo dessert in the Piazza Navona. Then gird yourself for an unpleasant trek so you can later depart on a pleasurable journey where you'll experience novel tastes, observe sights only previously seen in a textbook or a documentary, and maybe make the acquaintance of other intrepid explorers who, like you, have been cooped up too long.

Travel is what you make of it. Things can and will go wrong. You may have a guide whose accent is so thick you can't understand a word he says as he explains that the building was erected during the "medium ages." Instead of bemoaning his poor communication skills, figure out what he's trying to say. Maybe he means "Middle Ages?" You may have a city you were looking forward to visiting that is canceled entirely because of a stormy sea and your flexible captain will determine another port, a safer one, to park. Besides being grateful that your captain isn't a reckless adventurer risking your life and limb. Be happy that you'll now encounter an unexpected venue, which may turn out to be as good as or better than the original scheduled stop. Maybe you catch a cold aboard the ship, or on a tender, or from a crowded bus, and now you must forfeit an excursion, which you paid $100.00 for. It could be worse; you could be the old woman who fell off the bar stool and broke her ankle while she tried to consume enough alcohol to make the wine package worthwhile. And what about all that blood on the bricks where the tender pulled up? What if you missed a step and ended up bloody in a foreign hospital talking to a doc with the same command of English as that guide at the archeological park?

Perhaps you didn't like the sad songs the entertainer sang in the lounge? Then, stroll outside and admire the glint of the moon on the waves of the water. Your dining companions want to discuss politics, and their worldview is diametrically opposed to the way you feel. So what? Order another plate of escargots and overindulge your sensory taste buds in savoring the flavor. And tune out your other senses, like your auditory one. You didn't have a chance to purchase a souvenir on the quick-paced excursion you'd signed up for? Hey, the terminal building has shops. You'll find something.

No Wi-Fi? Read a book. Not feeling like dancing in the lounge. Write your impressions of the day or the other dancers. I saw one who looked like Fabio, only he had long white hair and was Canadian. Don't feel like participating in the trivia contest, that name-that-tune competition, the cooking demonstration, or anything they offer for entertainment? Soak in the hot tub. There's always a solution. There's always something to feel grateful for, even if it's just the smile of a helpful young employee who lends you a strong arm as you disembark a shaky tender.

And when you're at the airport to fly home and go through three long security checkpoints in Rome, be grateful when you get on the flight, and a tiny non-talker is sitting next to you. And you get to watch Nick Cage's wonderful film The Unbearable Weight of Massive Talent, plus two old Elvis movies: Viva Las Vegas and Jailhouse Rock. All while jetting home. Then you land in Newark and see a restroom before the customs wait, and you make a spry run for it. You find yourself in a stall when a commode nearby flushes and a torrent of water floods the floor like lava running down onto Pompeii. What to do? Hasten out of there as women scream: "My new shoes are wet. Oh no, my purse is soaked." Be thankful you were smart enough to hang your heavy purse on the handle on the back of the door, and furthermore, you were practical enough to wear old sneakers. When you retrieve your luggage every piece, even your husband's are revolving around the circular belt. Rejoice!

You've had fun. You've learned some things. And you realize there's always a price to travel that has nothing to do with dollars and cents but everything to do with attitude. When you exchange your currency for another country's, also exchange your Judge Judy spectacles for a cape of flexibility.

If you can't go with the flow, don't go.

(Psst! I'm no longer talking about toilet mishaps.)

-Erika Hoffman

FAMILY: LIVE, LAUGH, AND LOSE YOUR MIND...

Like Seriously Mom- Could You Not?

Of Cannibals and Mice

W HEN MY DAUGHTER WAS 14, she was in an advanced academic program at school, active in theater evenings and weekends, and prone to insomnia. The night before a major exam, I found her awake and anxious. I jumped to the obvious conclusion that she was worried about the exam, and she confirmed there was a small chance she might only score 95% if she didn't spend the next two hours cramming. I immediately launched into my "it's not about the marks" speech, followed by my lecture on "work/life balance". (Yes, I know, my parenting style was perhaps a bit too lecture-oriented, but I *was* a university professor, so... yeah.) I was about to launch into my "need-to-stop-cramming-and-go-to-sleep-so-you'll-be-well-rested-for-the-exam" speech when my daughter interrupted to say that it wasn't about the exam at all. Cramming was just a way to keep her mind off what was actually worrying her. I immediately jumped to the worst suspicions. *Oh no, did that creepy kid in the theater group try something on with her? I knew that jerk was going to be trouble*!

"One of the kids at school was showing this video."

Oh no! That sounded bad. "Yes? It's okay. You know you can talk to me about anything. I'm here for you."

"Cannibals. It's kind of freaking me out."

Not where I thought this was going; and not a problem for which I had a ready-made lecture. I was somewhat incredulous.

"You're not seriously telling me you're afraid cannibals are going to break in while you're asleep and attack you?"

She held up her thumb and index finger separated by a hair. "Little bit."

She allowed the fear was irrational, but couldn't get over the feeling there was someone hiding just out of sight, waiting for her to go to sleep.

I recognized the cannibalism motif was simply the lightning rod for a generalized existential panic brought on by ridiculous amounts of homework, too much extra-curricular activity, and all the social challenges of adolescence. So I sat down on the edge of her bed and started to talk her down by taking her fears seriously. I pointed out that (a) our house had a good alarm system to alert security if any cannibals attempted unauthorized entry; (b) our large black dog would immediately attack any intruders, and they would be the ones eaten, not her; and (c) I would be sleeping right upstairs and would hear if she cried out. She acknowledged this was all true and reassuring and she showed signs of maybe calming down enough to sleep. At which point the aforementioned large black dog burst into the bedroom, smashed into the wall, and tore her shelving apart to get at a wicker basket there. The dog in psycho-killer mode.

As one may imagine, this was not entirely conducive to the calming tone I was trying to cultivate.

A moment later, a tiny jet-black mouse made a break for it, sprinting across the floor and out the door, while the dog gave murderous chase. From behind me, standing on the bed, I heard my daughter shrieking, "I knew it! I knew there was something in here with me!"

"Well, it's gone now," I said, trying for damage control. Before I'd even finished the sentence, the dog was back, attacking the wicker basket once again.

I grabbed the damaged basket away from the dog, but before I could put it out of reach, I saw another (this time gray) mouse racing frantically around the basket as I inadvertently tipped it. Being the macho, heroic protector I am—I shrieked loudly and dropped the basket. The dog plunged her head back in and proceeded to smash the remnants to kindling in an attempt to get the terrified creature. Jaws abruptly snapped shut, and the dog trotted out of the room with the deliberate gait of an executioner.

Behind me, my daughter shouted, "Don't let her *kill* it! The mouse did nothing wrong!"

As I mumbled something about mouse trespass and the death penalty, I followed the action outside the bedroom in time to see a bullet-fast mouse (I was unclear if this was a third individual or if one of the previous two somehow escaped from the jaws of death) scuttle under the sitting-room piano—and my 60lb dog kamikaze into same nanoseconds after. As I called the dog back from battering the piano pedals, I felt my little night-time pep talk could definitely have gone better.

This was not, I am sorry to confess, the only problematic encounter with mice in the house. On another occasion, I had set a few traps to catch suspected intruders in the kitchen, with reassurances to the children that it was a 'catch and release' program. This worked relatively effectively, actually setting a few mice loose in the coulees, until I noticed one trap had inexplicably disappeared. Assuming I had just misremembered where I placed it, or that the dog had nosed it away somewhere, I forgot about it. A couple of days later, I was playing with my younger daughter in her room, when she reached behind her into her stack of stuffies to pull out—you guessed it—a dead mouse. Unfortunately, her collection of stuffies included three plush and somewhat realistic mice, so we both sat there staring at the dead mouse for 10 seconds before realizing that this one was *real*. (Well, the attached trap should have been a giveaway.) Why the mouse had dragged itself and the trap all the way across the house to my youngest's bedroom and buried itself in her stuffie collection, I will never know, but her reaction was predictably hysterical.

Still, could have been worse. Could have been cannibals.

-Robert Runte, PhD

Dad's in the Attic with the Brownies

I WAS AT THE advanced age of ten when my sister and I learned there were Brownies living in our attic. While I suspected there was no Santa Claus, Easter Bunny, or Tooth Fairy, my sister, who was only five, still believed. So, it came as a surprise to me then to learn about the existence of real magical creatures.

For those who are no longer children, Brownies are related to elves, pixies, and leprechauns. They usually live and play without being noticed by grownups, who pay no mind to anyone shorter than two feet, anyway.

This explains why my sister and I were shocked when our dad said he actually met some Brownies; although, he didn't know much about them when we quizzed him. By contrast, my sister and I knew quite a bit about them because we read about Brownies in a Golden Book we got one Christmas. That's when I had to pretend it was from Santa Claus for my sister's sake, even though I knew for a fact my mom bought the book. We learned Brownies were really small, around the size of a stuffed teddy bear, with hairy-looking pants and oversized green shirts. They always wore brown, pointy hats on their heads and talked in a kind of squeaky, singsong voice.

We realized that some stories we read weren't real. Like dolls that could talk to each other while we slept. But some of them could have been true we reasoned, like the Brownies. After all, they reminded us a lot of our friends. They just wanted to have fun and eat whatever they wanted—never okra or spinach—and play harmless tricks on people like hiding dad's extension ruler or mom's lipstick. Mom and Dad used to blame each other for hiding them, but my sister and I knew who really did.

Brownies were so unlike my dad, who never seemed to relax. He worked diligently as a tradesman during the week, coming home to eat dinner, read the paper, watch the evening news, and then go to bed. Boring. That was our impression of his life when we were kids. There was the occasional job around the house for him as well—taking down the screens and putting up storm windows in winter; taking down storm windows and putting up screens in summer, and other totally monotonous chores. It was when he installed an exhaust fan in the attic ceiling to cool the house in the summer that we learned there was more to the world than even we knew. That's when Dad first met the Brownies, but he said it was too risky for us to go into the attic and that we'd have to wait until we were older to meet them.

One time we overheard Dad telling Mom that our house was "infested" with them. We realized then they must have been responsible for all the creaks and cracks that we heard and saw in the house. We never voiced our suspicions for fear Dad would ban them from the attic and we would never be able to meet them.

In the interest of full disclosure, I have to explain we were the same kids who were thrilled we could have a pet goldfish. I remember how we raced home from school to feed it and watch it swim for about two seconds before switching to Captain Kangaroo on television. The last time we saw Shark, the goldfish, it was on the floor flopping around—trying to escape its tedium, no doubt.

One night, as I cleared the table after dinner, I overheard my dad telling my mother, "Well, I think that peppermint spray finally did the trick. All the brown pests are dead."

"What? You killed the Brownies?" Horrified, I dropped a dish on the floor.

My dad was startled and gave me a quizzical look that slowly turned into recognition. He had forgotten he told us about the Brownies who lived in the attic and that we could meet them when we were older. My sister, hearing all the commotion, ran back into the kitchen. I explained what happened: "Dad killed the Brownies." She began one of her marathon crying scenes. She was always blubbering about one thing or another so none of us paid any attention to her.

"Not the Brownies, girls, the bugs. Unfortunately, the Brownies ate them and got sick, so they decided to leave. They are definitely still alive. They told me they were tired of penthouse living and were seeking something more, uh, down to earth."

My sister and I were furious! He promised we'd get to meet the Brownies when we were older and now they were gone. Our anger surprised him. He had no idea his "brilliant" daughters were, in fact, living in a fantasy land.

Like many disappointments in life, we eventually got over this one. We grew up and forgot about the Brownies, along with the talking dolls, stuffed animals, and one goldfish we once cherished. Our childhood home was sold a long time ago and its present residents have no clue about its former physical or metaphysical occupants.

After my dad sold the house, he moved to California—not far from Disneyland, where the idea of charmed, magical beings isn't so crazy. He, ever the creature of habit, installed an exhaust fan in his attic soon after he moved into his new house. The last time I saw him he complained that his tools just seemed to go missing and then he'd find them in the oddest places.

"Brownies, Dad?" I asked with a smile. He laughed, shook his head 'no,' but then he became contemplative and, in a quiet voice, asked if he had ever told my sister and me the truth.

"About the Brownies?" I asked, and as foolish as this sounds, a part of me held my breath and hoped for a different answer. He looked at me seriously without confirming or denying my question and then changed the subject. His hearing loss was acute; still, Dad did have a mischievous sense of humor. There still is a part of me that wonders if there had been more to the story of the Brownies in the attic than he revealed. It's hard to let go of a deep-seated fantasy.

You know the expression, 'bats in the belfry?' Well, my family now says 'Brownies in the attic' to explain when a special object, like a cut glass olive dish or a painting on velvet, goes missing. Still,

I remain convinced that someday I will climb into a future attic and find those rascals. I'll keep you posted.

-Marlene DeVere

Secret

MY HUSBAND AND I were expecting our second child. We made our announcement to our family over lunch at a busy Olive Garden. As expected, my parents and sister and his grandmother, aunt, uncle, and cousin broke into wide smiles and loud cheers.

As we did with our first pregnancy, we wanted to keep the news just within the family until the three-month mark - a month and a half away. Everyone agreed to our request.

A week later, I dressed in a silk sari with a matching necklace, earrings, bangles, and a bhindi on my forehead. My husband and I arrived at an auditorium to listen to a South Indian music concert. My husband's family attended as well.

Before the concert, the audience socialized. As I was taking my seat, a family friend, Deepa, excitedly told me she was going to be a grandmother. Her daughter was expecting her first baby. I matched her excitement by asking about the due date and how her daughter was doing with morning sickness. Soon after, the audience took their seats, and the concert began.

Sometime during the evening, Deepa bumped into my husband's grandmother, whom we call Paatti. Deepa, giddy with her happy news, told Paatti that she was going to be a first-time grandmother.

I can imagine what had happened. Paatti with her small frame draped in a green sari and her gray hair pulled into a tight bun, would have tried her best to keep our secret. But as Deepa went on and on about expecting her first grandchild, Paatti would have felt the need to one-up her. Like a tenuous dam trying to hold back as the pressure mounted with each word Deepa uttered, Paatti would not have been able to contain herself.

In the end, she blurted out that she was expecting another great-grandchild. Then, after the moment of superiority passed, the guilt gnawed at Paatti.

As soon as Paatti got into the car after the concert, she confessed to my husband's aunt that she told Deepa about my pregnancy.

My husband's aunt was mortified. She had to remedy the situation. She hurried back to the audience, who were milling outside the concert hall, and hunted down Deepa. My husband's aunt spotted her and took her aside. "Don't tell anyone that Viji's pregnant."

Whew! Damage control was successful!

Months later, when I was well into my pregnancy, my husband and I heard the story. We could not help but fall over laughing because Paatti had spoken to Deepa Rajan and my husband's aunt had spoken to Deepa Kumar. Only in our family!

-Viji K. Chary

Bad Day with Garlic

I CAN NEVER FORGET my Bad Day that involved garlic.

My Father-in-law was an energetic, curious, brilliant, and elegant 6'4" (1.94 meters) man in his 60s with bright blue eyes with thick silver-styled hair in those days. He had pages worth of skills. A corporate insurance adjustor by profession, and an engineer by natural skill; my Father-in-law could do everything from transmitting Morse code to building a canoe and restoring two British sports cars.

I could not have married my city-born husband if a barn hadn't been promised to me. My husband, better known to me as Sweetie, said in the spring he would rent an excavator and put in a water line to the barn.

Sweetie announced that the next Saturday he would rent the excavator and his dad would come down to help with the project. My Father-in-law was always so eager to help us. I found out only he would come, and he would be there for the afternoon and supper. My Mother-in-law was another multi-talented person, and he was used to eating meals fit for magazine covers all the time. I spent hours looking over recipes on the computer and consulting my older female friends for this important occasion. I found a recipe for Chili con Carne.

The kitchen was my mom's domain at my first home. I had no interest in learning, and she had no interest in teaching. She cooked with stuff she knew and liked. There were some ingredients that were simply avoided including most spices and especially.... garlic. There was NO garlic in the house and to bring "that" in would have been like asking for a rattlesnake for a pet.

Sweetie introduced me to garlic. I found that we both loved the "forbidden" vegetable that was so good for us because it just made foods taste that much better.

I had a recipe found for Chile con Carne. Sweetie showed me how to use his garlic press in the kitchen. All I needed was garlic from our local grocery store.

I went to the store, and I had to read the signs until I found the one that said "Garlic". I always envisioned it more as a scary-looking tentacle, like a stringy angry form of celery. Never had I even looked at, much less picked up, this "forbidden" thing before. Remembering I needed two cloves, I went through them, selecting the two biggest I could find. I wanted this supper to be perfect.

Plunging the pieces of garlic into the press and grinding it to come out the bottom was my next job. I was not even halfway through what the recipe called for when my eyes started to water, and my head felt strange. I was feeling fine before this and while anxiety was gnawing at me for this big supper, I knew these symptoms as I had them before. *OH NO, I thought, oh, please, not another allergy*!

My eyes were now blurry with tears, and I was dizzy. Halfway there, I could do the rest, I HAD to! I was determined to not let my Father-in-law down. The recipe clearly called for two. I now KNEW I had a garlic allergy and that made me sad. I had my last three pieces to go when Sweetie came in the door and said in a loud voice, "WHAT are you doing? The windows are closed. I can smell garlic OVER the diesel fumes of the excavator by the barn!"

I looked up at my new husband. My eyes full of garlic caused tears; I told him I was sorry that I had a new allergy. He then explained to me that a clove was a SINGLE piece of the garlic bulb. I was working on my *15th clove*.

We debated what to do next. We decided to put the fans on in the bathroom and over the kitchen stove and threw open all the windows. Maybe my Father-in-law would not notice and besides, he liked garlic, Sweetie said

I watched for my Father-in-law's arrival in the next hour. He pulled his brand-new minivan into the lane. I had time to get the fans off and a few windows closed before he came to the door on this bad day.

My Father-in-law came to the house and came inside. He first smiled at me and then, looked a bit startled. He then slowly said, "I won't be staying for supper, just so you know. I don't want to drive back home tonight in the dark."

-Cathy Hamill-Hill

Mom

I T WAS 7 A.M. on a Tuesday in 2007, back when I was 12 years old. I was at the point of maturity where I was trusted to begin my day in solitude but needed a once-over by my mother to ensure that I was set to get on the bus. I made a pepper, bologna, and cheese-filled omelet for breakfast with the accompaniment of MTV music videos in the background. My mother finally emerged from the hallway in a black muumuu, with rollers barely clinging to her hair. I glanced at the clock, and it was 8:05 a.m. Normally around this time my mother would ask me if I had all my books, make sure that my shoes matched, and watch me as I left for the bus stop. However, my mother was distracted by her current weight loss journey. So, I hung out at the dining room table while I waited for the bus to arrive.

The bus driver I had throughout the majority of my pub-lic-school experience was a woman I respected. She would punc-tually arrive at my stop at 8:15 a.m. and would greet each child with a smile but ensured with an iron fist that no one was harassed or bullied by another student. Now, I am not stating that my bus driver would ever hit a child or apply any physical force, but.... she had a tendency to approach whoever was being problematic and "accidentally" fall on them. Now, if you are imagining a petite 5ft 2inch blonde woman, you would be mistaken. Ms. Oak was around 5ft 10in (1.78 m) and had the build of a retired line-backer. This woman had no problem literally throwing around her weight to protect whoever needed help. And if you're think-ing students could verbally harass each other or go through any extreme name-calling, you are mistaken. While driving, Ms. Oak would gladly call out a child and indirectly insult them to end it.

It was finally 8:10 a.m. I put on my shoes and grabbed my backpack. My mother finally decided that today was ab day. She moved the coffee table back, loosened her bra, and went to light a candle to cover the smell of sweat. The poor bath and body candle she chose for the day was a favorite of hers. The wick was all the way at the bottom and there was ash around its opening. To compensate for the lack of lighting surface area (on the wick) my mother grabbed some pages of yesterday's newspaper, crumpled them up, lit one end, and tried to light the candle. I guess the breeze from the front door being opened killed the flame instantly, so my mother had to up her game. My mother grabbed an arsenal of newspaper and hairspray...something in my gut told me I needed to take a few extra steps away from my mother. When my mom lit her chemically drenched wick and paper, flames shot up higher than when the fireworks blasted Shan Yu in *Mulan*. My mother rushed over to the candle with oven mitts, the fire extinguisher, and went straight out the door.

My stomach dropped as the school bus stopped in front of my house while my mother fought flames in her black, sweat-stained muumuu, hair curlers dangling in the wind, and her bra at her ankles. I heard Ms. Oak tell the kids to stop trying to take pictures while chuckling herself, and slowly pulling the bus away from the curb.

-Karl Stevenson

How Can I Embarrass You Today?

M Y DAUGHTER, KELLY, WAS the literal child. This is the child that when I said, "Watch your mouth!" pulled her bottom lip out and looked at it with crossed eyes. I didn't have to do anything TO her for her to be embarrassed by me. On days I ate lunch with her at school, she pleaded with me at the door, "Please don't embarrass me".

And of course, I gave her the innocent look (that I learned from her).

Six-year-old Kelly looked at me, closed her eyes and paused for a minute as if to wish she could drop into a deep hole. After the dirty stare, I followed ten paces behind her as I had been instructed. Once we sat down at the table, waiting for her friends to join us, she began with a heavy sigh as she prepared to give me a "list" of things I was not allowed to do. She began...

"Don't talk while you eat. Use your fork. I'll introduce you, so you don't have to talk and ask my friends silly questions. Are you really wearing that?"

Sigh.

"Don't pick at your food or your teeth, and if you have to say anything, don't say it loud."

"May I nod?" I suggested. "Can I buy a vowel?"

It's hard to have a good time as a frozen statue, only nodding at little people, knowing Kelly was scrutinizing my every move. But we managed a lunch date at school.

Needless to say, I minded my manners and spoke in a low tone so as not to embarrass her. I didn't pick my teeth, nor did I blow my nose (yeah, she forgot one). I behaved, and she even thanked me for coming and suggested we do it again.

"Sure, if I don't have laundry to do!"

My oldest daughter, Morgan, was the exact opposite. She introduced me to her friends, encouraging me to talk to them, asked if

I enjoyed my food and said that she couldn't wait until I came for another school lunch visit!

"This is MY mother!" she said proudly and enthusiastically.

Kids spend most of their time embarrassing us, assuming their embarrassing moments towards us don't count. According to them, we aren't allowed to even the score. However, we do, whether we mean to or not. Without a doubt, the day comes when we inadvertently embarrass our kids, even the ones that don't merit it. Morgan, the delighted child, really didn't deserve to be embarrassed by her mother. Although, I was sure it was forever etched on Kelly's mind, the day that I drove through the school car rider line with...trash bags on top of my car.

I had taken a nap and woke up to find it time to pick up the kids. It was sanitation day (which I had forgotten). So, hurriedly, I hoisted a couple of full trash bags on top of the car and by the time I got to the top of the driveway, with the kids on my mind, totally forgot about it and zoomed on down the road to pick them up from school.

The car rider line was long, as were the faces of the people we passed as the line moved. When I pulled up, my kids didn't want to get in the car. I yelled at them to hurry and get in as teachers standing around started writing things down while walking back into the building. I'm sure my poor kids were put on some kind of "watch list" that day. As we drove off, people quickly backed against the wall on the sidewalk. My kids were so mortified they didn't mention the trash bags until we got home.

Looking back, it was memorable. That's all it was. Memorable. Well, shocking and memorable.

To this day, my daughter Morgan, who is now thirty-seven years old, reminds me of that day when I mention picking up children from school. Even her childhood friend, Wendy, still remembers, and they laugh at my expense.

Curious, I asked my daughter Kelly what she remembers about that day. She replied, "Mother, I only vaguely remember that. I think I must have blocked all those memories out of my mind."

Well, imagine that. At least my grown kids are still entertained after all these years. And I'm still trying to figure out how those trash bags defied gravity to do it.

-Debbie Gibbs McCoy

Surprise Birthday Dinner

W HEN I WAS A busy mom with two school-aged children, I had a lot to do and a lot to keep track of, which kept me on the move most of the day. Even in the summers, I kept my son and daughter busy with some schoolwork to keep their brain in shape, lots of music practice, and lots of fun time with friends.

On top of all of that, I had plenty of housework to complete and healthy meals and snacks to prepare.

Sometimes, I functioned on autopilot.

One summer, when I was busier than usual, my brother-in-law decided on the morning of my sister's birthday to have an impromptu surprise dinner.

He called me from work and gave me all the details. Piattis, an Italian restaurant at 7 o'clock.

"It's a surprise," he said. "Can you tell Amma and Appa?"

"I'll tell them," I said.

As soon as I hung up with him, I called my parents. They didn't pick up the phone, so I left a message.

I went on with my day

A few hours before dinner, my brother-in-law called me from his home phone.

"You blew it! You ruined the surprise!" he said.

"No, I didn't. I didn't tell her," I insisted.

"Listen to this," he said.

He played a message on his home answering machine. I heard my voice.

"Hi Amma. Nupoor is having a dinner for Purnima tonight at Piattis at 7 o'clock. I will see you then. It's a surprise. Make sure you don't tell her."

I was confused. How did he get the message I left for my parents?

Like a blurry picture slowly coming into focus, I realized what might have happened.

Could I have really dialed the wrong number?
I could hear my sister laughing in the background.
Shoot! I could and I did.

-Viji K. Chary

Hoist the Hatchet! It's Grandma!

I TRIED TO READ as I sat on the plane for my trip home to Seattle from San Francisco. Was I the same person who seized every opportunity to read but couldn't concentrate on her book? Why?

Why? I scheduled a flight at the break of dawn so I could return for Grandparents' Day at my grandsons' school. That's a crucial commitment because the teachers release students from class when grandparents attend. Released from class? Being released is what that day is about for them. Do you know a kid who wouldn't fire his grandmother if he missed that opportunity?

The flight's schedule changed, and the earliest flight I could reschedule was at 10:00 a.m. That sent worry waves up my spine, but I told myself that all I needed was to arrive at school in time for my grandsons to claim me after lunch. That's when the students race into the lunchroom, and eager grandparents scoop them up.

I observed worried glances as I twitched on the plane and wanted to shout, "Have patience with me. I'm an at-risk grandparent!"

When my perspiring body arrived in Seattle, the mother of my grandsons, who would have their hatchets poised if I didn't show up on time, whisked me to school. I jetted out of the car, abandoning my daughter, and arrived in time to see a stream of dependable, smiling grandparents leaving hand-in-hand with grandchildren. Those same worry waves declared a field day on my spine.

I raced inside to find the innocent faces of my boys, in sparkling white uniform shirts, smiling as they gleefully table-hopped to pilfer leftover desserts. I raced to them and sputtered apologies. Downing their booty preoccupied them, but eventually, they acknowledged my existence and consented to take me to view their classrooms. No amount of praise for their artwork gained my clemency.

Whoever said I needed to be a grandparent, anyway? I did. Those squirts are my *raison d'être.*I could not repeat this grandparent debacle.

A few weeks later, I went to another grandson's kindergarten project day. He read to me the book he had written and illustrated. The pleased smile on his beaming, open face captured my heart—again. I ate the pancakes my son volunteered to cook, hugged my grandson, and left to retrieve my car—a perfect, on-time grandmother.

No car. I traversed endless blocks, hunting it down. It was an SUV with three juice-splattered, raisin-dotted booster seats and the receding smell of one grandchild's vomit. Who would have stolen this vomitorious vehicle?

There was a parking enforcement person and I begged him to help me locate this car that I'd give anything (except a grandchild) to find. He scouted the area, returned minus the car, and asked me if my car had locators. Of course, it did! I called my vehicle's roadside assistance. The operator said that I needed both the car's VIN and a police case number in order for them to locate the car! It wasn't too far to walk home to ferret out the VIN in my records, but a police case number? That meant reporting a crime. A crime?

I considered enlisting help from my son who was still at the kindergarten cleaning up the pancake feast. Why not have him circle the neighborhood? Why not? Because I'm his mother who might just be losing her marbles. Before my mother died, we banned her from driving children because she was a risk to my grandchildren and herself. Was history repeating itself? It was one thing to lose my car. It would be another entirely if my children sent me to THE HOME. I was not calling my son. I didn't want him to even think about it!

I conceded defeat and called in a police report. They took my information, but they wouldn't give me a blasted case number. A police officer needed to check out the situation. Now would I ask my son to drive me home? My son was kind and loving.

That wasn't the point. This was salvation from the home. I walked home, even though my heels were far from walking shoes. Sore feet were the price of silence.

About an hour after I arrived home, a pleasant police officer in blue serge and brass buttons arrived at my door to give me a case number. This burly guy and I chatted companionably about his upcoming retirement. He left with marginal evidence of dementia that he had been surreptitiously scrutinizing and said he'd scout for my car.

Half an hour later, he phoned. He had my car! I collapsed with relief in the nearest chair. My life could resume. Then I shot up from the chair when he told me they found my car about one block further than where I recalled having parked it. I fumbled with an apology and swallowed my shame. Relying on the officer's good nature, I asked him if he could take me to it. He agreed. Officer Friendlies are not a myth.

On our way to my car, the officer handed me his phone to show me pictures of his retirement house. And then we found it—luminous in the sunshine, my underappreciated SUV giving me a second chance. I thanked the police officer with a box of candy I had stored in my freezer and popped out of the cruiser. The officer gave me a knowing glance. I had his phone in hand. He asked my size for the straight jacket he would order for me. Given that option, I returned his phone. Thank the heavens for Officer Friendlies and my under-appreciated SUV.

-Marcia McGreevy Lewis

My Daughter Channeled Ethel Merman

MY DAUGHTER CHANNELED ETHEL Merman when she was little, barking out her uncensored observations in decibel levels capable of cutting through any acoustic barrier. I was horrified.

On one occasion, when we went to the grocery store, Amelia and I were standing at the checkout counter with *several* other customers.

Amelia yelled, "Mama, I just love your BIG SMOOSHY BUTT!" while burying her face straight into my bottom.

Another time, we were sitting at a small table in the center of a restaurant dining room, surrounded by other patrons.

Amelia shouted out, "Mama, what color is our—"

Let's just say it was an uncensored word she shouldn't be shouting out in public. Especially when what she really meant to say was *Volvo*. Like our family car. Which was green, by the way.

Now that we are both older, my hearing is bad. I bark out my caustic observations, oblivious to their decibel level, and it is my daughter's turn to be horrified.

Once we were sitting at the bar in a cocktail lounge, along with a few other individuals.

I *enthusiastically* told Amelia, "That man is LOOKING AT YOU."

"Mom, you are talking really loud."

"NO, I'M NOT. AM I?"

Shaking her head, Amelia replied, "Mom, do you think this is funny?"

-Jill Egland

Always a Surprise

I T WAS THE AFTERNOON of my birthday when I received the best birthday surprise I could have ever asked for. I was going to be a mom!

It was a true surprise.

You see, a couple of years earlier my husband and I learned we would not be able to have children on our own. We had spent the years since trudging through the adoption process. We had just switched a couple of weeks earlier to a new adoption agency after having gone through a couple of failed adoptions and *so* much time waiting.

As I sat on the couch waiting for my husband to return home so that we could celebrate, I received an email from our adoption case manager.

A prospective birth mother had picked us, and the baby was coming in just a couple of months.

We got to meet the prospective mother the next week.

Within a few minutes of meeting her, I noticed something.

The baby NEVER stopped moving in her stomach.

I had been around plenty of pregnant women before. Several sisters, friends, and coworkers. I had even seen their babies kick and move. But never had I seen the baby move constantly.

Throughout the entire meeting, it was like her stomach was the ocean, waves flowing back and forth. The only difference was that the waves of her stomach had a lot more feet and hands trying to press their way out.

This little boy never stopped.

We met her a couple more times before the birth of our oldest son. And each time we met it was a challenge to not stare at her dancing belly.

For some reason, once our son joined our family, we were surprised by his need to still always be moving.

As a young baby, he *always* needed to be moving. Whether being rocked, walked, or in a swing.

He ended up crawling, walking, and running at very young ages.

He was always on the move. Even in his sleep.

Once he was a toddler he could easily climb out of his crib. But he moved so much in his sleep that we kept him in the crib, otherwise, he would fall straight off the bed.

One day I heard him wake up from a nap in his crib. I had to rush to get him out once I heard him so that he wouldn't climb out on his own. The moment I opened the door he stood up on the frame of the crib and jumped—

I ran to catch him, but being on the opposite side of the room... I didn't make it.

He landed with one hand extended out, supporting all his weight.

He cried for a moment but quickly moved on with his day. I watched him over the next couple of hours. Though still playing around like normal he kept looking at his wrist where he had landed. He wouldn't let me look at it or check it out. My gut told me something was wrong, and I decided to take him to the doctor.

As we sat in the waiting room my son was all over the place. No one would ever guess he was hurt in any way. The doctor was going to think I was crazy to bring him in.

I wasn't wrong about that.

Right as my son started doing a handstand, the doctor came in. As I explained my concerns about his wrist, the doctor stared between my son and me trying to hide his disbelief.

My son wouldn't let the doctor examine his wrist either, so he ordered an X-ray to "rule out a break". It was most likely just bruised and tender, or at most sprained.

After 10 tries to get a picture of my wiggly boy's arm, the X-ray was done.

Again, we found ourselves waiting in the room for the doctor to return. This time I stared at my son in disbelief as he ran, jumped, and climbed around the room. *What was I thinking? He really is fine. What a waste of all our time.*

As my son grabbed the doorknob to try and escape from confinement, I overheard the doctor and nurses talking.

"I can't believe it really is broken!"

"You owe me $10."

Not only had my son really broken his wrist. He broke it in two different places.

It never slowed him down. He would still move and move.

Always a surprise.

-Amilee Weaver Selfridge

THAT ESCALATED QUICKLY...

Stirring Up a Hornets' Nest Just to Make Friends

I NEEDED A FRIEND or two. I was a stay-at-home mom with two girls: Sarah, who was seven years old, and Lauren, who was one year old. In 1996, we had the internet, but it wasn't like it is now, so I didn't really have any way to connect with other mothers my age.

One day I found an ad in our local paper looking for moms of young kids to join a Moms' Club. I was excited and called the number to RSVP.

The day finally arrived. I had my diaper bag packed with everything needed for the day and we headed out. The woman who had advertised the club was named Charlotte, and the event was at her house not far from me.

I'm a shy introvert, so it took a lot for me to put myself out there. But everyone I met was warm and welcoming. Some women were already members and talked to me about how much fun it was to be part of. A little later, I was walking with Sarah in the backyard while holding Lauren to my shoulder. Suddenly, a huge hornet flew by me, and I waved it away. Then another one landed on me, stinging my arm. I cried out in pain and fear, but before I could get away, hornets flew at me from all directions, getting caught in my long curly hair, and going up inside my shirt.

Sarah screamed for someone to "please help my mommy!" My eyes were closed so they wouldn't get stung, and I clutched Lauren to my body and leaned over, hoping she wouldn't get hurt. I was about to get on the ground and cover Lauren with my body when I heard a woman's voice yell for me to give her the baby and then run for the house.

I thrust Lauren away from my body, hoping someone was there to grab her. Thankfully, there was. The hornets were stinging my back, my neck, my ears, and squirming and buzzing in my hair, making it difficult to run. My screams sounded as if I were in a horror movie (which I *was*), and finally, I had to pull my shirt off and flung it into the grass where hornets clung to it and crawled around it. I ran my fingers through my hair to dislodge the bees angrily caught in it.

Finally, I made it into the house and into the kitchen, my bra straps down around my arms. Angry red welts rose on my skin, snot dripped from my nose, and tears streamed down my face.

Charlotte covered me with a towel. "Are you allergic? Do I need to call an ambulance?"

I shook my head no, then looked around. "Where are my girls?" Sarah was sobbing and hugged me when they brought her from the living room. Lauren was asleep in a port-a-crib.

A couple of women applied Benadryl to my stings. Someone brought me water, and others just stood around and commiserated.

It was one of the worst days of my life, not only the hornet attack but also because I had to tear off my shirt in front of a couple dozen strangers. Which strangely, was the most horrific part of the day since I'm such an introvert. I ended up staying. Someone grabbed my shirt after getting rid of the hornets. After I cleaned up and got dressed in the bathroom; I signed up for group activities, Sarah played upstairs with other kids her age, the babies gurgled at each other on the floor, and I finally got to chat with women, some of whom would become good friends over the next couple of years.

That night, Charlotte called me to make sure I was okay and to apologize. I told her she had nothing to apologize for, but she said that earlier that morning she and her husband sprayed the yard because they knew there was a nest of ground bees. I happened to step into that area while they were already enraged, so they took it out on me.

Although I find the crazy incident funny now, I developed a fear of flying insects. If I hear a buzz near my hair, even if it's just a fly,

I'll freak out. Sarah, now in her 30s, developed a bee phobia as well. Thankfully, Lauren never remembered a thing.

I'm still an introvert, but that story has broken the ice for me many times over the years when confronted with the dreaded "Tell us something about yourself!"

-Sheri White

The Party

W E'VE ALL BEEN TO a lot of parties in our lives, some best forgotten, but one comes instantly to my mind. In fact, it makes all the other parties I've been to pale into insignificance as far as memories go.

We lived at Mt Colah, in Sydney's far north when our children were very young. It was a happy community, populated by young couples like ourselves, who had bought cheap houses and land packages from the many shady developers that sprang up in Sydney during the late sixties and early seventies.

So parties were a regular event, with the families in our street each taking it in turns to host.

One Saturday night, we found ourselves at friends who were rich enough to have a swimming pool.

Things were going well; our three children were enjoying the rough and tumble with the other children from the street. They tired themselves out swimming and playing with the numerous dogs and cats that followed their owners to the party house.

As darkness fell, I decided it was time to bed my three young kids down. John drove our station wagon into the yard and parked it in a corner behind the pool. Well away from the house so the loud music would be somewhat dulled, and they would hopefully go to sleep.

Wonder of wonders they did, and John and I settled in to relax and enjoy ourselves when, suddenly, distant sirens could be heard. I wasn't sure at first if I was imagining it, but within a minute or so they became loud enough to drown out even Johnny O'Keefe, who was raucously telling us "I'm a Wild One" via the spinning vinyl.

Everyone stood still to listen in surprise and our host opened the blind and exclaimed in amazement, "There's a heap of police cars coming up the road, lights flashing and all".

We couldn't hear what he said next because the cars screeched to a stop right outside the house.

Most people raced outside to see what was happening. The sirens were turned off as the police opened the doors and dropped to their knees beside and behind the cars.

"Stay down, get inside, stay away from the windows. There's a mad gunman in the street, get inside, quick, don't stand there gawping, get inside and get down."

Most people were more interested in watching the spectacle than doing what the police were yelling, but all John and I could think of was our kids–asleep and down the backyard.

We raced out to find our way blocked by two burly policemen, guns drawn and looking worried.

"Get inside," one of them yelled, "didn't you hear?"

"Yes, but our kids are in the car," I pointed to the station wagon, "I'm not leaving them there."

"They're safer there than anywhere. There's a young man with a gun, he's shot his father and run into the bush, we're expecting him to come out about here."

They might have been safer where they were, but no way were we going to leave them by themselves. Followed by a torrent of abuse from the police, we ran to the car and jumped inside.

We lay down on the seats near the children. They were still sound asleep as we listened to the chaos that ensued outside.

The police ran into the bush behind the house and we could hear the moment when they found the offender.

Frighteningly, we discovered the next day he actually ran through our backyard. We found plants trampled and footprints in the garden beds.

But back to the party. It continued well into the early hours, with several policemen returning to join us when their shift ended. They told us the father had survived his son's rampage and also told us they thought we were a crazy bunch to have so completely ignored their orders, however; they said our party looked like the best place to be in Mt Colah after their nightmare of a shift.

I'm sure it was.

-Jill Baggett

Alligator Spiders

M Y SISTER GUELMARI, MY nieces (Elena and Lucia), and
I visited Universal Studios, Orlando. I know I am being
disloyal to my adored Walt Disney World (my love place) but,
Harry Potter. No need to say more. We had a magnificent weekend
filled with magic wands, butterbeer... and it was free! Guelmari had
four tickets to the parks, including the hotel. My brother-in-law,
away on a business trip, could not use his so... Girls Trip!

When told I would join them, Lucia says, "See Titi?" She gives
me an important and serious look. "See why you should never get
a boyfriend? So, you can always be with us!" It is not the first time
she shared her thoughts on my love (or lack thereof) life.

On the way back to Miami, Guelmari is driving. The roads are
clear. It is a beautiful, sunny day. The girls are quietly reading Harry Potter books in the back seat. With a smile, I am daydreaming,
reliving one of the best weekends of my life while I try to spot
alligators and sip on a cold Diet Coke. Life is good.

Suddenly, the car is full of piercing screams and wet crying.
Lucia howls like a banshee, "There's a giant orange spider on my
door!"

Elena, even louder and trying to escape her seatbelt confinement, "It's poisonous! The orange ones are poisonous! I learned
that in school!" (Great. Excellent moment for an Arachnology
lesson.)

This information makes Lucia panic. "It's going to kill me!"

The back seat is chaotic. Guelmari looks at me with imploring
eyes. "Hermana, do something!"

Because Wonder Woman has nothing on me, I put my soda in
the cup holder, unhook my seatbelt, climb over the seat, Converse
in hand, jump over a sobbing niece, and, after several attempts
(the sucker was fast!) smush the spider. (I feared the "poisonous"
creature too, but the nieces do not need to know that)

Silence. Only the sniffing of drippy noses and the relief of being rescued are heard inside the car. I am back in my seat with shoes on my feet. Everything is in order. After a few minutes, Guelmari speaks: "Hermana, did you have to leave the mess on the car door? You could have picked up the spider gently with a tissue instead of using your shoe..."

Right. Because at 70 miles per hour on Alligator Alley, with two screaming nieces and a runaway arachnid, my concern was where to leave the spider's corpse.

I wonder if all the other superheroes get asked these kinds of questions.

-Marta A Oppenheimer

New Year's Day Key Chain Follies

WHEN MY KEY CHAIN split, spilling keys like pick-up sticks on the hallway's hardwood floor, I took action. I headed for the only hardware store open on New Year's Day, where I chose a replacement, a sturdy oblong one with a rounded screw post. Little did I know or care that this overqualified key chain had been adapted from its original use.

Outside the store, I came to realize that the holes in the bow of my apartment unit key, and in my building fob ("the small hand-held device that controls a remote keyless entry system"), were too small to slip over the rounded screw post.

I thought to enlarge the plastic fob's hole at home, with hammer and nail, so I put it safely in my wallet. Then, I got impatient and tried to force my apartment unit key onto the screw post. Not surprisingly, the key got bent—like a magic trick on tv—and became clearly unusable. (Had I inserted it in the apartment door lock, it would have broken off and caused even more trouble by orders of magnitude. Even I wasn't that stupid.)

Next, while walking home, I took my wallet out to make sure the building fob was still there—and watched with horror as it seemingly leaped and executed an arabesque midair, before landing on the sidewalk, after which it skittered like a rock on a pond only to disappear into a sewer grate. Buh-bye!

I was now locked out of both the building and the apartment—and out 50 bones, the price of a replacement fob.

Miraculously, my long-suffering wife answered her phone (she almost never does) and was in a charitable enough mood to head-shakingly let my sorry self in.

Two days later, I came upon the word "carabiner" in a poem. Apparently, that's what the D-shaped coupling used by rock climbers but later also adapted as a key chain is called. On the first day of 2023, I had bought myself a carabiner that, in short order, made me its plaything by turning my life into an outtake without the cameras rolling from an old Jerry Lewis movie.

-Kurt Lipschutz

Push It Real Good

IT WAS MY THIRD day in Germany. I would live there for the academic year as an optional year abroad for my university degree. Already, I had pretty much changed my mind about doing the year abroad. I didn't want to be away from my love and family and friends. Anxiety a constant boil in my stomach. The days had been a mishmash of tears, shaky hands, and rapid bowel movements (sometimes simultaneously).

When in Germany, it is customary to collect bureaucratic documents, in the same way one might collect autographs or stamps. German administration is a labyrinth. I was terrified of getting something wrong and being deported before my time there had even begun. My first few days there had been stressful, consisting of navigating papers A, B, and C on top of my crippling homesickness and nerves.

That day, I went to a Very Important Building in search of a Very Important Document. Said building was five floors high, in the center of a student quad with a cafeteria on one side and an ancient Egyptian history building on the other. The door to the building was a massive metal monstrosity. With two hands, I flung it open. I arrived around half an hour before closing and was surprised that the inside of the building was dark, gray, and silent. I convinced myself they closed early. Then the metal door slammed with finality and the anxiety that had been bubbling for the past few days exploded.

My gut twisted as though I urgently needed the bathroom. I pulled on the door and the hinges rattled teasingly, but it did not give. Each slam echoed around the building. *Maybe I should call to some students for help? Would I have to spend the whole night on the floor?* Like a toddler in desperate need of a wee, I tottered from foot to foot, wondering what to do and willing myself not to cry. Then my eyes fell upon a button beside the door. A button that would release the door. My savior. I jabbed my thumb on the button. There was a delicate tinkling noise. It was so delicate it was mocking the alarm bells that began wailing in my head.

And throughout the building.

The building became alive with a pulsating whee woo whee woo siren. I did what I should have done to begin with, and found somebody. Up five steps, I encountered a delightful, middle-aged, bald man who looked as panicked as me and assumed I was in some kind of danger. I hastily asked him if he spoke English and explained my accident. Another man appeared and led me down the stairs. He shoved the door open easily and attempted to prop it open, but it kept swinging shut. I was vindicated; the door was not cooperating with him either.

The first man came out of the building and, like the second, attempted to prop the door open. Then, without the screaming sirens, I could explain how I ended up pressing a mystery button. I swear, I thought it would open the door.

Not only had I set off the fire alarm, but I, being the polite British girl I am, held the door open as the five-story building evacuated. As each staff member hurried, confused and nervous, out of the building, I apologized in English and kept saying there was nothing to worry about (I didn't know how to say it in German).

The two men who got me out of the building came back over with a woman whom they introduced as their boss, to whom I had to explain the situation. All three of them were wonderfully polite as I explained I just arrived in the country and was feeling incredibly overwhelmed and had a moment of panic. The fire alarm echoed. The occasional tear escaped me, but I swallowed everything down. I couldn't stand any more embarrassment. A crowd was forming, made up of both evacuated staff and students from the cafeteria.

"The door was stuck?" They asked me. They were surprised at my claim.

Once everyone evacuated, the first man went back inside, shut the door, and flicked it open as though dredged in butter. The brief vindication I had vanished in a finger snap. I had an awful realization. I apologized even more profusely, blushing and tearful.

"It's okay, it's alright." They laughed in exasperation.

They couldn't call the firefighters off, so we had to wait for them to arrive. Once again, being the polite Brit I am, I asked the boss of the building if I should stay around to explain what happened, but she and the men waved me off and told me I could go. They hoped they wouldn't get a fine for wasting the emergency service's time. Guilt pooled inside me. I needed to go back to my flat, calm my shaking hands, cry, and urgently use the toilet.

After all that, I didn't even get my Very Important Document. I would have to go back and face them all the next day. Luckily, the man told me which floor to find it on. At least I'd evacuated the correct building.

I walked away, and I could hear another kind of siren, faint in the distance, but growing louder with every beat of my heart. The fire engines. *They were very prompt.* German efficiency. Like birdsong, the sirens overlapping each other. It sounded like there were at least two, if not three. I debated running back to my flat and hiding under my blankets forever or simply flying back to England.

I called my mum instead.

She answered right away.

"Mum, I've just made an idiot of myself!"

She thought I had done something small and forgettable, like trip in public. She was rather shocked when I held up my phone to the chorus of sirens with the declaration that I had somehow managed to evacuate a whole building. Back in England, she was howling with laughter. I laughed too and cried at the same time. I had reached my limit and was somewhat hysterical.

"It happens to everyone." She said. "We've all almost accidentally set off an alarm before."

262 THE BAD DAY BOOK

"Almost is the keyword, Mother." And that set her rambling again.

The alarms were stronger.

And the worst part of it all: my realization.

I had set off the fire alarm, evacuated a five-story building, disrupted staff members' work, potentially caused them to face a fine, and wasted the valuable time of firefighters.

All because I was pulling at the door.

And it was a push.

-Hannah Mitchell

The Body

"You should get one of these," she gushed.
"It'll make you look so slim.
It'll bring you down two sizes or more.
It hides a wealth of sins."

And so early the next morning,
I headed out to buy one.
I found one on a hanger and rushed to try it on.
An item of black spandex that would revolutionize my life.
Make me look just tiny.
Chisel me like a knife.

In my haste to buy this item,
in my urgent need for procurement,
I didn't see that on the fourteen hanger,
there hung a size eight garment.

I rushed into the changing rooms
where it felt a little muggy.
I stripped off all my clothing
and stood there feeling chubby.
(For those who are wondering,
and before I hear you snicker,
for the sake of decency,
I left on my big knickers).

The cubicle was warm and stuffy,
and I started to perspire
as I tugged on this item
that I thought my body required.

It was tricky to squeeze into it.
It took a very long time,
but it would be worth the effort
to make me look sublime.
I tugged and shoved and pushed.
I pulled it to and fro.
I fastened up the poppers located down below.

And finally, it was on,
but it did feel rather tight.
Yet I tried hard to convince myself
that it made me look alright.

I gazed in the mirror at my size fourteen bod
squeezed into this tiny lycra thing.
It all felt rather odd.
So, I hummed, and I hawed
and decided against the option
of constricting my body inside
this new-fangled concoction.

And so, I tried to take it off,
but it was proving rather tricky.
It wouldn't budge an inch.
I started feeling horribly sticky.

I unfastened all the poppers
and tried to lift it over my head
but the lycra gathered around my waist
and became completely wedged.
I tried to ease the item down
and roll it to the floor
but the lycra became all scrunched up
and would move no more.

And so I stood there nearly starkers,
panicking, sweating profusely,
with a rubber tire stuck around my waist
which I pushed and pulled obtusely.
Nothing happened, nothing moved.
It was totally and utterly stuck.
There was nothing I could do.
I was completely out of luck.
Time was ticking slowly by,
but I couldn't leave the booth
Because if I did, everyone would see
the awful ugly truth.

A middle-aged woman
with a tire stuck around her belly.
An ocean of fleshy flab, a stomach full of jelly.
My mind was working overtime,
searching for ways to set me free.
A huge pair of scissors would cut me out,
but everyone would see.

I couldn't even contemplate
the thought of such humiliation.
The shop assistants smirking at the body extirpation.
I could hardly request some scissors
without explaining the cause:
my self-imposed imprisonment
in the midst of menopause.

A tiny voice in my head encouraged me to be resolute
and to remove this wretched body of ill repute.
And so slowly, almost imperceptibly,
I eased the item off me.

Millimeter by painstaking millimeter,
I tried to shift it softly.

Without exaggerating, it took close to forty mins
to work my body out of my new found second skin.
The result of the effort left me like a quivering wreck.
Trembling, humiliated, totally drenched in sweat.

When I finally removed the body,
I got a huge surprise.
Because that was when I noticed
I'd picked a tiny size.
The ridiculous situation that I'd been in
made me snort a laugh.
How could a sensible woman
commit such a stupid gaffe?

I quickly put my clothes back on
and legged it out the door
resolving never ever
to go back to that store.

-Nuala McEvoy

My Fear of Snakes

OPHIDIOPHOBIA: THE FEAR OF Snakes

I have ophidiophobia, a fear of snakes. 1/3 of people share this fear. It is innate for mammals, of which we are, to be afraid of snakes.

My fear dates to my childhood, last century, when my younger brother would put plastic snakes in my bed. I would pull down the cover, scream, he would jump out of the closet, laughing and yell, snakes.

I am now protected against snakes by my husband, retired Air Force Captain, otherwise known as the OICSS–Officer in Charge of Spooky Stuff, or Officer in Charge of Sneaky Snakes. I am the food and laundry fairy.

This division of labor worked without a hitch until April 2019. The OICSS had a total knee replacement from a military injury. He had to abdicate the throne and guess who the OICSS was now? Yes, me. The OICSS reassured me before surgery that he sent a message to all local snakes to stay out of our courtyard. He needed his wife to be rational and in control during his recovery. Thanks, OICSS, for putting snake city on your pre-operative checklist.

2 weeks into his recovery, the laundry fairy was at work. At 10 a.m., I paddled outside with a basket of laundry and stopped dead in my tracks. There, bathing in the sun, drawing a line between me and the laundry room, was a 3-foot snake. I was about to scream snake city for the OICSS to rescue me, but realized I was the OICSS. I quickly changed my tune from screaming in fear to frozen in fear. "Hi, snaky poo. I need to do laundry and I really need you to disappear, but do not slither into the house." I whispered to the sneaky, slimy snake, "please go right now," as if the snake understood English. The snake obviously understood

and slithered into the rock garden. Well done, OICSS, now back to laundry. No time to think about snake city.

Two days later, out in the courtyard, I was again greeted by snake city. My prior attempt at sweet talking the snake obviously unsuccessful. Maybe, if I opened the front door of our courtyard leading to the outside, the snake would depart from this fine Boca hotel. Slowly, I crept around the snake. I opened the front door, and stood aside. I was in begging mode now. "Please snake, the exit is here." By now, my eyes were bulging, arms waving frantically, words running fast out of my mouth. "Please, snake, exit now, the highway sign is lit." The snake understood and promptly headed to the open courtyard door, but not alone. Another 4-footer, slithered out of the bushes and the couple, obviously in love, slithered away. I screamed, Snake City. I had a snake city living in my courtyard. Breathe, breathe, you are the OICSS. Don't pass out – having one disabled person per household is enough.

I am happy to say that OICSS fully recovered and returned to snake duty.

December 2020, snake city revisited me. After homeschooling our 5-year-old granddaughter, the OICSS and I were playing with Play-Doh. Grandpa made a Play-Doh snake and threw it at me. I screamed snake city and jumped up from the chair. My granddaughter, as only an innocent 5-year-old would do, came up to me, looked me straight in the eyes, touched my arm so gently, and said, "Grandma, it is only a pretend snake. Pet this snake, Grandma. It is pretend." She was so correct. Not only is this a Play-Doh snake, but I do not want to instill in her my irrational ophidiophobia.

Thank you, sweet granddaughter, for reminding me of the huge difference between real events and pretend. Listen to the words of the children as these words are true and priceless.

Thank you, OICSS, for accepting my irrational ophidiophobia and protecting me against snakes.

Every day, I still wonder, did that snake couple leave behind snake eggs to repopulate this snake city? Only time will tell, as I will keep a vigilant watch when I step into my courtyard.

-Dr Marlene MD

A Tale of Ruined Khakis

M Y HUSBAND, RICH, WORE the same few outfits for years—at least ten, sometimes longer—because he didn't like to shop. "There's nothing wrong with this shirt," he would say when I commented on the thinning elbows of his long-sleeved dress shirt or when I complained that the grass and oil-stained trousers should no longer be worn in public. "They're small spots," he protested. "No one will notice."

Well, I noticed; and I was afraid people would think I never did his laundry. So, one day, when his entire wardrobe of pants (three pairs) had "just a few small spots," I finally convinced him to go shopping. At the store, he reluctantly tried on summer-weight khakis and after trying on only three pairs, he found some that fit. I was relieved that my mission was accomplished.

Rich wore them for the first time when we went to visit friends. He was still wearing them later when I served dinner and when a meatball escaped his fork. His new khakis became a canvas of abstract art.

"I can get that out," I said confidently and scurried to the laundry room to work my magic.

My Aunt Judy, who knew more about laundry and housekeeping than anyone I'd ever met, always swore by bleach for removing all kinds of stains on any and all kinds of fabric. So I liberally applied a bleach pen to all the saucy splotches and popped the pants into the washer. When I removed them from the washing machine an hour later, voila, the red spots were gone; replaced by white spots.

Not wanting to admit to Rich I'd ruined his new khakis, the khakis I'd convinced him to buy, I devised a new plan. I would buy khaki-colored fabric paint to cover my mistake. I hid the damaged pants in a place he never went (the laundry room) until I had time to sneak away to the craft store.

Unfortunately, the craft store was out of the color I needed, so I bought khaki-colored acrylic paint instead. This should work, I thought. I took it home and applied the paint to the largest white splotch. Hmm, the khaki-colored paint didn't match the khaki-colored pants. Maybe when it dried, it would, I thought. Who knew there were different shades of khaki? The painted area was more noticeable than the bleached areas.

Well, maybe a permanent marker would cover up the white spots. I found a light brown marker in my arts and crafts supplies and carefully dabbed color onto another bleached spot. That didn't match either.

I rewashed the pants. The spot I'd painted and the spot I'd colored with a marker both faded to different shades of beige.

But all was not lost: I had a new idea. I returned to Hobby Lobby to purchase fabric dye. Later, after I'd dyed the pants a beautiful dark brown, I planned on telling Rich how my ingenuity saved his $30.00 slacks.

In the meantime, Rich continued wearing his old pants, not even questioning what happened to his new pair. He probably wanted to prove he hadn't needed new ones in the first place.

Armed with a mop bucket filled with warm water, I meticulously followed instructions for mixing the chocolate-colored dye. I stirred the pants for twenty minutes. My arm got tired, but I was determined to follow the guidelines and save those pants. They would no longer be khaki colored, but they'd look good with his brown and green plaid shirt.

When the timer went off, I drained the water and rinsed, then drained and rinsed repeatedly until the water ran clear. I wrung them out and held them up to admire my work. The khakis had turned a rich, lovely brown, just as I'd expected—except where the bleached spots had been. Those areas were beige. But at least all the spots were the same color of beige.

I realized I'd have to confess to Rich that I couldn't repair his new khakis. Fortunately, he has a sense of humor. We giggled over

272 THE BAD DAY BOOK

my misguided efforts to redeem them. "That's okay," he said. "I like pants with a giraffe pattern."

He wore them around the house but still didn't have a decent pair to wear in public, so we went shopping again. This time we bought two pairs. He wouldn't have to shop for at least another ten years.

Sometimes life is like this tale of ruined khakis: No matter how hard we try, we can't fix some of our mistakes. All we can do is learn from them. And laugh at ourselves in the process.

That's what Rich and I do whenever he wears his giraffe-colored pants.

-Diana L. Walters

Vroom vroom... Wait

A FTER A LONG DAY'S work, I spent my evening with my partner at the time who had warmly welcomed me into his home. We had a nice, peaceful time; we watched some Netflix, ate some of his mother's leftover spaghetti, and then I absolutely destroyed him in *Mario Kart*, as usual. When the evening came to an end, I got into my car and went home to have a good night's rest... is what I would've said if things went as expected.

When the evening came to an end, what actually happened was, I said my goodbyes to my partner and left his house, only to come right back in. I assumed he was playing a cute prank on me to make me stay a bit longer, but when I asked him, *"Alright, where's my car?"*

With a look of genuine concern, he replied, "What do you me an..."

In the couple of hours I was at his house, my car was taken right out of his driveway, never to be seen again.

He was kind enough to drive me back to my house. I made some calls as soon as I could, hoping my car wasn't gone forever. It wasn't particularly expensive, in fact, it was fairly run down, an eye-sore, even. Why someone would steal such a car baffles me to this day.

I slept terribly and once I managed to get my eyes to close and my mind to drift, a phone call woke me right back up. 5 a.m. They called to say they couldn't locate it, but at that point, I cared very little about their apologies and lack of findings. I was much more worried about the three hours of sleep I had left to have before I had to find a way to get back to work.

One hour is all I ended up getting. I woke up to a text from my partner saying he would drive me to work today if I needed. I gratefully accepted. As I went to leave my house, I realized I had left my favorite shoes in my car. I had only bought them a month ago. Now, if I wasn't upset about the car, I definitely was about the shoes.

I got into my partner's car, sulky, but once we passed the gas station, I snuck a glance at the price, remembering I was due for a refill. Yikes. Maybe it wasn't so bad not having a car.

I'd be using my former gas money to buy those shoes again.

-Allay Rei

Who Do You Think You Are Talking To?

I HAD TO BABYSIT my friend's twins for a few hours. I barely knew them personally and hadn't spent any alone time with them, especially without their mom. It means the same thing, they never spent any time in my home, with or without their mom. Also, I already had my toddler to care for.

Only 2 years ago, I hadn't ever spent any time caring for kids.

Here I was, actually taking care of 3 (the 5-year-old twins, one girl, a boy, and my toddler) AT THE SAME TIME.

I was so worried; I wasn't sure whether to clean the house before they came or not. What if they messed up everything and refused to clean?

I decided to wait to do the chores and keep an eye on them at all times. What if they split?

I locked all the other rooms and kept them in the living room. Luckily, my house was divided in two ways. To the right of the main door were two bedrooms and a bathroom, while the living, dining, and kitchen were on the left. My small office was near the living room, visible from the main door.

The morning started, and my right eye flickered with worry as I knew something was going to happen.

The twins walked in with their backpacks. Their mom thanked me profusely and confirmed that she would return in a few hours.

I locked the door and peeked to check if all the bedrooms and bathroom doors were locked.

Walking a few steps to my living room. I found the kids on the couch. They had removed their backpacks to sit on the corner ends with a book each. Nice! This must be the quiet before the storm. My toddler, who was always near my legs, joined them too. They seemed to like each other's presence.

Maybe it wouldn't be as bad as I thought. I massaged my right eye and sat on my computer chair.

Taking advantage of the opportunity, I read my To-do chores list, which was kept on the computer table.

First on my list was clearing the clog in the bathtub drain. The couch was to my left, and I could keep an eye on the kids from my computer table.

So, I switched on my desktop and put in a request for maintenance on the portal. Voila! First job done!

I looked at the happy trio. The twins were on their second book, and my toddler sat in the middle to read or pretend to read his. I smiled and crossed my fingers, hoping for this to continue.

Second, on my list was to make arrangements for an upcoming family trip. Since my computer was already on, I searched for all the free things to do during the trip. The kids stayed put, with my toddler in the middle.

After half an hour, I was almost done with my itinerary when the doorbell rang.

My son would typically hide behind me, but he saw the twins continue reading their books, and he did the same.

Opening the door, I welcomed the maintenance guys inside. It surprised me they were so prompt. I knew Frank and Steve well, as something was always off in our 75-year-old building, and they frequently visited. Frank was the friendlier one, and Steve was a little silent. They couldn't see the couch or the living room from where they stood.

They walked five steps to the right-hand side of the house to enter the bathroom.

I heard metal clanking as I sat down on my computer chair.

Suddenly, like most kids do, the girl crept up behind me. She saw the screen and asked me the question that most kids ask a thousand times daily: "What are you doing?"

"I'm planning a trip." My right eye twitched. Maybe this is how it would begin.

"Where are you planning the trip to?" she asked meekly, looking at the screen.

"To a nearby island," I replied and noticed her head tilted as she seemed completely mesmerized by the screen. I broke her spell. "Sweetheart, you're too close to the screen. Can you scoot back? Maybe sit on the couch again? I can still answer you. I'll be loud."

She thankfully followed instructions, and I cleared my throat, ready to talk loudly. "Who will you be going with?" she asked as she climbed on the couch again.

"I'll be going to the island with this little monkey and his father," I said, pointing to my toddler.

They giggled softly, and she asked, "Where will you stay?"

I saw Frank take a peek at me. His eyes were wider than usual, but he was smiling. He didn't say anything, and returned to the bathroom to resume working, as I heard metal clanking again.

"I'll be staying in an Airbnb." Before she could ask me another question, I said, "Looks like you are done. Why don't you clean up, and I will tell you more."

There was pin-drop silence for some time as they packed their bags. Even the maintenance guys were quiet. I found the perfect place to stay within our budget and sent the link to my hubby to check.

I decided to give the kids a snack before starting the third task. Happy with my progress in caring for kids and chores, I asked cheerfully, "Would you guys like a snack?"

Three kids nodded. As I was about to get up from my chair, Frank walked to the main door, looked at me, and said, "Thank you. We don't need a snack."

"Oh!" My face flushed with embarrassment. I smiled and pointed to the couch. "I was talking to the kids."

He walked four steps into the living room until he could see the couch and the three kids sitting there, who looked at him blankly.

His hands immediately went to his forehead, and I saw the red color rise on his cheeks, too, as he mumbled, "Oh, there are kids here. You were ... oh, that explains a lot."

It was then I realized that he probably didn't hear the meek voice of the girl but heard my loud voice and thought I was talking to him all the time.

As realization dawned on both of us, we couldn't help but laugh. Even Steve chuckled from the door. What a day!

-Sunayna Pal

Expect Turbulence: The Post-Breakup Flight That Had Me Laughing

I woke up on my ex-boyfriend's futon, rubbing the sleep out of my eyes as my ex stood over the stove, cooking. It took me a second to realize that this wasn't a bad dream. I had been dumped the night before, capping off a trip across the country to visit my then-boyfriend of over two years. Apparently, he wasn't feeling sparks between us anymore, which soon left us staring at each other in silence over breakfast.

Over a plate of bacon, I asked if he had been faithful to me. He said he had, but it was of little comfort to me, the Californian who'd just been broken up with on the East Coast.

He drove me to the airport, and we sat in silence for the whole ride. When we arrived, he hoisted my luggage out of the bed of his truck, hugging me with a heartfelt "goodbye" before driving away.

I was relieved that in just a few hours, I'd be home, free to cry, and eat chocolate and blast all of Taylor Swift's best breakup songs a little too loudly. But, like my recently failed relationship, it wasn't meant to be.

I boarded the plane to Chicago. Unlike every other moment from the past 24 hours, the flight was uneventful, and I thanked the universe for my smooth travels. With a three-hour layover before my flight to Los Angeles, I figured I'd have plenty of time to kick back and relax.

About an hour into my layover, I was in the middle of inundating my friends with all of my relationship woes when I noticed my gate number had changed. Armed with an overflowing purse, a heavy backpack, and an oversized suitcase, I trudged to my new gate, hoping that I hadn't left anything behind.

Shortly after, I went to a nearby eatery to purchase a salad when I realized my ID card was nowhere to be found. I frantically rushed back to the gate and searched every row of seats. Nothing came of it. I scoured the floor and asked others to join my search, but we all came up empty. Then, a thought occurred to me. I must have left my ID at the original gate.

Desperate to find my ID card, I hauled all my belongings to the gate I was originally assigned. I searched meticulously, like I was surveying some type of crime scene, but I still came up short. I reported my card to the airline's lost and found and gave thanks that at least I had my passport on me.

After heading back to my gate, I amused myself by watching the arrivals and departures board — until my flight changed status. Suddenly, without warning, my flight was delayed by an hour.

Time ticked on, but that didn't seem to matter. My flight's arrival time stretched further and further away until it became clear that I might be too late to catch any transportation home after I deplaned in Los Angeles.

By this point, I was in tears, silently cursing every little thing that led up to my flight delay. I may have been a 26-year-old woman, but I was in serious need of some comfort, so I called my mom.

My mom, whose kind but assertive presence had worked miracles on countless customer service representatives, suggested I speak to the woman at the front desk of my gate. I asked if the representative knew of any other flights to LA, but there were none to be had. My mother decided that she wanted to speak to the airline representative via speakerphone, and I obliged. She asked the woman if there was any way I could get home tonight, but the representative said that just wasn't possible. I spent several minutes apologizing to the representative, apologizing to my mom, and trying to find solutions. Ultimately, though, we realized that the only way to get home that night was for my parents to make the hours-long drive from LAX to our home themselves. It wasn't at all convenient, but it would have to do.

Hours after I originally planned to board my Los-Angeles-bound flight, I finally was ushered onto the plane. The plane had nine seats in each row, and the layout left me flummoxed. I navigated a maze of airplane seats, but I finally found my assigned spot. By this time, I was too tired to even think about having a chuckle at my laughably terrible day. I sank into my seat, cracked open a bottle of lemonade, and took a big swig, hoping the sweetness would take the edge off some of my frustration. (It didn't. I spilled lemonade on my pants as the plane was taking off.)

In the middle of the flight, I was daydreaming about curling up in bed when I heard the distinctive beeping of the "seatbelt on" light. An announcement came over the speaker: "Due to inclement weather, the plane will soon experience extreme turbulence. Please fasten your seatbelts now."

Suddenly, I felt the plane drop rapidly. My heart beat out of my chest, and my stomach knotted up. The acceleration pushed me upwards, and I felt like I was tethered by nothing but my seatbelt. It seemed like the plane was falling out of the sky. I joined a chorus of passengers' screams, fearing I would soon die a fiery death. *I'm not dressed for a water landing, and I'm an awful swimmer. How will I survive if the worst happens?*

The plane's jolting seemed to last an eternity. When it finally ended, though, I nearly burst out laughing. My day seemed almost comical. I was broken up with, I lost my ID in the depths of O'Hare Airport, my flight was delayed multiple times, and the plane experienced so much turbulence that I was convinced we would be forced to land in the water — all in under 24 hours.

Thankfully, the plane remained stable for the rest of the flight. I collected my baggage without incident, and I made it home safely. As I crawled into bed, I realized that the worst day of my life was also one of the most memorable. Sure, I no longer had a boyfriend or an ID card, but I now had a ridiculous (but completely true) story to tell at parties — and a renewed sense of survivorship, too.

-Kelly Douglas

It's Only Just Begun

I HAVE ALWAYS LOVED reading. The older I got, the more I began enjoying the escape I found while reading fiction. It was all fake. When the characters were hit with problem after problem, I didn't have to worry about the stories triggering my personal stress because the problems they faced weren't problems I would deal with in real life. It was all fake. I mean, an entire book would have hundreds (if not more) of dramatic challenges for the characters to get past, usually only in a couple of weeks. Bad times just aren't like that in real life. Or so I thought...

Near the end of my time at college, I had a wonderful group of friends. Over time, one of these good friends started having romantic feelings for another.

He told the girl. Only she had no idea, so when she (that's me) found out, she was like...no.

Time passed and he (my smart future husband) didn't give up. He wore me down until I realized I couldn't live without him.

First came love, then came marriage.

Marriage to me has always been a two-parter. First Marriage 1.0, the act of getting married; and then Marriage 2.0, the future spent together...married.

So, first came Marriage 1.0.

At 10:00 p.m. the night before my wedding, I found myself frozen inside my mom's car at the car wash. Apparently, washing your car in frigid winter temperatures isn't the smartest choice. But I found there was no better way to spend my last night single than with my mom laughing in the dark parking lot until the car defrosted enough to drive.

I woke up the morning of my wedding to excited butterflies in my stomach; only to realize they weren't butterflies, and whatever it was, definitely wasn't excited.

Instead, I spent my morning trying to get ready while battling the urge to throw up. But I made it, and only ten minutes late!

Which didn't matter one bit when we found out our officiant wasn't there. In fact, because of a miscommunication, he had never even been notified of the wedding.

My future husband and I sat together and waited for over an hour and a half. Laughing together while our growling stomachs kept getting louder and louder.

The day kept going in this fashion. My name was said wrong during the vows, our pictures were taken outside in weather under 10 F (-12 C), me in a short-sleeved dress, the camera malfunctioned causing us to go in and out of the cold repeatedly for pictures, the drama between others, and worst of all... being too busy to not eat the Crème Brule I had looked forward to most. Well, besides my husband, of course.

But as we walked into our new home together late that night, I was exhausted and happy. Despite it all, it was perfect.

We were married and our time together had only just begun!

Naively unaware that, for better or *worse*, literally began as soon as the vows were made.

We advanced to Marriage 2.0.

So here we stood in our new apartment, a new life ready to begin.

And we had our first argument. Or so I thought...

You see. We both had work the next morning. Because of some scheduling conflicts, we ended up getting married two weeks before the end of my now husband's college semester. We wouldn't be able to go on our honeymoon until school was out. And being poor college students, we could only miss so much work.

Which left us standing there arguing whether we had time to open a couple of our gifts before heading to bed. Okay, really what happened is I said we should open a couple of gifts to celebrate our marriage. My husband said let's open just one. So naturally, I opened three.

Then we set our alarms for 6:00 a.m. the next morning and went to bed.

I was sure being tired at work would be the hardest part of the next day, but really it was fending off all my coworkers asking me why on earth I was at work; the day after I got married.

At least after the workday, we would get to spend the weekend at home together. Even if my husband would be busy with end-of-the-term schoolwork and studying.

But the second night after our wedding, I woke up to my husband moaning in pain. He had a persistent pain in his side that kept getting worse and worse. After a couple of hours, we needed to go to the hospital.

Here it was 6:00 a.m. and I was on the phone with my mother-in-law, getting insurance information to head to the hospital.

At the hospital, we learned my husband had a kidney stone. And that he is *extremely* entertaining and honest under the influence of heavy medication.

They sent us home, my husband still heavily sedated with pain medication, for him to pass the stone at home.

The next day was a low-key day. Him still recovering and joking that we must have hit our limit to the drama. This was real life, not some fantasy book. And really, what more could happen?

Well, the following morning at 6:00 a.m., we once again found ourselves at the hospital. Only this time, it was my turn. That stomachache I woke up to the morning of my wedding, had continued to get worse and worse. I found myself once again wishing it were only butterflies. Instead, it was a pocket of stones filling my gallbladder.

I would need surgery. Luckily, even though the stones were painful, they weren't an immediate risk. We could wait a week so that we could go on our honeymoon.

We already paid, and it was our honeymoon. We didn't want to cancel.

I spent the rest of the week not feeling great, while my husband finished his semester.

Then we finally got to go on a *vacation. (*I use that term lightly here.)

My husband spent the first night and the next day taking his final exams in the hotel room. We then went to Disneyland where my husband pushed me around in a wheelchair admiring all the rides I couldn't ride on and eating yummy corn dogs I couldn't eat.

We decided we would go home, complete my surgery, and then we would begin our real Marriage 2.0. The first two weeks had just been a fluke.

My surgery took place on December 23rd. The next 24 hours are what we call "unspeakables." The kind of bad that isn't funny and has no reason to be spoken of.

Fast forward to our first Christmas together. We didn't really spend it together. My husband celebrated with my family while I laid in bed, not even caring that I was missing my favorite time of the year.

I ended up back in the hospital twice during my recovery. The challenges piling up.

But, luckily for me, my husband was there. He could take care of me and be with me.

He even moved our mattress to the floor of the tiny front room of our apartment and would spend the nighttime hours, when I was in too much pain to sleep, playing the new Super Mario Brothers game with me.

It didn't matter that everything was going wrong. We had each other.

Or so we thought...

Despite it all, years later, we look back at this time fondly. We reminisce about the funny moments we shared during that dark time. And laugh as we recollect the moment that through it all got closest to destroying our new marriage. Playing Super Mario Brothers.

Never, ever in our years together have we argued as much as we did when teamed up together to defeat that game. My husband constantly pulled ahead and killed me as I fell off-screen.

It helps me remember; any time you think nothing else can go wrong, it's only just begun.

-Amilee Weaver Selfridge

THE END IS NEAR

Don't fret!

This is not the end of bad days or of

The Bad Day Book.

Both will keep on coming.

Visit our website to find new books coming soon or to share your own bad day experiences.

Find us on 🔵   *Instagram*

Acknowledgements

I set out on a mission to create The Bad Day Book, but I never could have made it to this point on my own. Each of the following groups and individuals deserves a huge shout-out, plus heaps of praise and recognition for their part in helping The Bad Day Book come to life.

There aren't words to properly thank the many authors who joined with me to bring more laughter and joy to this world. They have shared not only their beautiful writing but parts of themselves. They put up with the many hiccups that came with creating this book series. From receiving emails at weird times of day (based on my schedule as a mother first), to the confusion caused when I had no idea what I was doing. Not only did they put up with me, but they were also always open to helping in any way possible. A wonderful group of individuals that I am happy to have worked with and hope to work with again. My newest friends.

Did you see our book cover and logo design? I connected with Jenalee Marshall in a local business group. She has been with this project from the very beginning. She listened to my rambling visions of what I wanted The Bad Day Book to become, and expertly put those visions into the designs that represent us. Flawlessly balancing what we thought we wanted with her personal design knowledge. Creating the perfect brand to be the face of our book series.

Most of us are adults, but this book would not be what it is without the pictures. The cartoons took the humor and level of this book up a notch. The different artists skillfully created pieces that help connect the readers to the stories they are reading. As a meme-loving society, I can think of no better addition to the book. Again, at times I was clueless when working with the artist. They graciously helped me and humored me throughout the process. A welcome addition to the project that I hope will continue through the long run.

I never would have thought of adding cartoons on my own. I was contacted one day by Van Scott, who runs a newsletter for cartoonists, suggesting that cartoons would be a good addition to the book series. And wow was he right? How lucky we are that he reached out. I am also grateful for his continued assistance in facilitating and working with our cartoon submissions for further books.

Outside of the glaringly obvious realization that I could never have gotten to this point on my own, I have been shocked by the relationships built throughout this process. These individuals are more than their stories or pictures put to paper. They are wonderful, real people. Individuals that I hope to maintain both business and personal relationships for the years to come. You never know when you are going to make new friends.

To each and every one of you. Thank you.

Artists

in order of appearance
Ali Solomon, Al Rozanski, Martha Campbell, Suzy Becker, Phil
Witte, Larry Miller III, Corinne Katow, and Harley Schwadron

Authors

in order of appearance
Jon Jones, Leah Mueller, Heather G Preece, Susan Helene, Kylie
Wang, Luke Pernotto, Ethan Freckleton, Tammy Brown, CLS
Sandoval, Bien Santillan Mabbayad, Victoria MacDonald, Don
Drewniak, Robert Runté, PhD, Nancy Julien Kopp, Braden
Lewis, Rosemary McKinley, William Craft, Becky Villareal, NRV,
A. C. Blake, Gary Koppel, Karl Stevenson, Dave Bachmann, Doug
Jacquier, K.J. Carter, Saul Greenblatt, Linda M. Crate, M.M.
Stansky, Maggie Nerz Iribarne, Teagan Durkin, Kelly Buchanan,
Lorina Stephens, Chiazo Obiudu, Bill Carrera, J. A. Norman,
Geary Smith, Hidayat Adams, Andee Baker, Erika Hoffman, Joyce
Frohn, Mandy Shunnarah, Cheryl Anderson Davis, Joyeeta N.
Chowdhury, Norma Gardner, L. G. Reed, Tony Elston, Marta A
Oppenheimer, Deva Shore, Ed Friedman, Mary Traynham, Larry
Perkins, Lucy Giardino Cortese, Sarah Elizabeth Das Gupta, Jill
Morgan Clark, Neil Ellis Orts, Diane Payne, Marianne Brems,
Vickie Goodwin, S.J. Walker, Jennifer Shneiderman, Jamaatun
Rohmah, Viji K. Chary, Elizabeth Spencer Spragins, Chuck Gas-
ton, Marlene DeVere, Cathy Hamill-Hill, Debbie Gibbs McCoy,
Marcia McGreevy Lewis, Jill Egland, Sheri White, Jill Baggett,
Kurt Lipschutz, Hannah Mitchell, Nuala McEvoy, Dr Marlene
MD, Diana L. Walters, Allay Rei, Sunayna Pal, and Kelly Douglas

Printed in the USA
CPSIA information can be obtained
at www.ICGtesting.com
LVHW022257200224
772404LV00028B/1001